The Black Man & His Visa

T0329442

Jean Tardif Lonkog

Langaa Research & Publishing CIG
Mankon, Bamenda

Publisher:
Langaa RPCIG
Langaa Research & Publishing Common Initiative Group
P.O. Box 902 Mankon
Bamenda
North West Region
Cameroon
Langaagrp@gmail.com
www.langaa-rpcig.net

Distributed in and outside N. America by African Books Collective
orders@africanbookscollective.com
www.africanbookcollective.com

ISBN: 9956-728-67-9

Introduction

When I completed high school at the age of twenty, I could not see the future I wanted. Everything was bad. I did not know the next step to take. I did not have the finances to enter university. It was also very difficult to enter any professional school here in Cameroon. The rate of unemployment was so high. In short hardly anybody was hoping for any good. Even university graduates had nothing to look for. Even when there were opportunities for work, thousands of people would flog there to compete for the rare places. The result was that the rich and those who had people in high positions in government would grab them. After a few years at home, I entered university and had to drop out again due to lack of finances. This book narrates how those difficult circumstances pushed me to travel to China hoping for a good life. As I migrated to China, I hoped to have a different life, a life better than the one I had in Cameroon. However, my expected good life cut short because my residential visa expired sooner than expected, and I had to go through difficulty after difficulty. I had thought life would become tranquil, peaceful and successful. But one thing kept me busy and constantly fearful: the visa, the visa. I finally learned that life is a struggle, as long as you are alive you cannot hide, and you cannot run away from problems. In moving to another environment, you can have a change of life, but in the new environment there are new problems. You will see in this book how I faced my own situation from the first day I entered China on 23 March 2005 until I left on 15 June 2008. I hope you will enjoy this little piece of work.

Jean Tardif Lonkog

1

Circumstances that led me to travel to China

I completed high school at the Cameroon School of Arts, Science and Technology or CCAST in Bambili in the northwest part of the country. I studied history, economics and geography. CCAST Bambili is a prestigious state school in Cameroon, and they admit the brightest students. As it is with most young men, I had many ambitions about my future. I had average grades, therefore I could have a place in any state university in Cameroon. At that time, one course of action occupied my mind: enter university, climb the academic ladder as far as possible, become a full time university lecturer. I had no money but had a kind of irresistible hope and urge that it was impossible to stop me. Never did I imagine that years would come to pass without me realizing my dream.

My father was a medical practitioner, an herbalist and a spiritual healer. He owned his own clinic in my hometown of Santa. There he treated and healed the sick. He was treating not less than eighty patients a day, therefore his life was not supposed to be miserable. He had many wives and children. In that case as in most African polygamous homes, it was difficult for him to sponsor us in school. At the time, his clinic was doing well, and he very busy. We his children were still young and still at primary school. We were doing very well in school. However, just a few years to the time that my brothers, sisters and I began completing primary school and started entering secondary school, he slowly and steadily sank into a kind of depression. He started drinking and could not sit steadily in his clinic. He would sit in bars, and when the patients or the sick came, we his children had to go around and call for him, "Papa, patients have come," and return with the reply, "Ok, he is coming."

He would go to the clinic, administer treatment, and return to the bar. His life was a daily routine like this. Most of the time he kept his drink before him without drinking, but he just had to sit there. With this kind of habit, naturally the clinic deteriorated and he could no longer raise any money from it. There was a problem too that he had a less business-like attitude, as most of the people he treated ended up paying him just with thank you. Then around 1998 he said like a joke that his time was over, "time pass." Slowly everyone forgot his real name. Most people knew him as "Pa Time Pass." At this time, each of my father's wives had to sponsor her children in school because he had nothing to offer. My mother had six of us. I have five sisters, and my uncle adopted one of my sisters. Therefore my mother, a peasant farmer, had to send my four sisters and me to school. This was not an easy task. She tried her best each time, until we graduated from high school. There was a big blockage after that. She could not afford to help us enter university. The burden was heavy on her and anybody could see this, for she always took loans at the village meetings. At times, it was too heavy on her to settle these debts.

By May 7, 1991, my father passed away at the age of fifty-two. The family missed him as a good and caring father. There was the psychological burden of living without a father. But our mothers did not experience additional burdens because for the past five years, they had been the ones sending us to school.

By the time I was completing high school in 1993, it was already too hard on my mother. It was clear that if I had to rely on her, I could not enter university. My sisters had to go to school too, at least up to high school, so my mother could not afford sending me to university especially as there was no university in my hometown or in my province as a whole. During this period when I had to stay at home, I worked hard in the farms hoping that somehow I could succeed in having a good harvest, selling it and entering university. However, most of the time I invested in farming, mostly market gardening, I never had good harvests nor good sales, at least not good enough to help me enter university. And I was unlucky for I suffered from disease. Malaria and typhoid fever attacked me permanently. Almost every month, I stayed at the hospital for treatment, sometimes twice a month. Then even the small money I earned from the farms I had to use to pay the hospital for treatment and good health. I needed strength and physical energy in the farms, but because I was always sick, the farms too failed.

Despite my health, I continued in the farms. In 1996, I hoped I could enough from them to enter university. I applied to read history at the University of Buea in the southwest region of Cameroon. I secured a place at the university, and I worked so hard in the farms to raise money for my studies. Despite much work, the money ended up not being enough, so I had to stay back again. I felt so bad. I had already stayed at home for three years and with no hopes. I could not figure out what the future held for me. How could I help my poor peasant mother who had worked so hard to send me to school? She gave all she had. All she harvested from her farms she sold for me to go to school. She had stayed without food for my sake. I saw how she strove to pay the loans she had taken for us at the village meetings. I saw how she worked day and night so we could go to school. My mother would go around and borrow money for hospital bills for me – an adult already out of high school.

There I was, sitting with her and watching her suffer. I could do nothing about it. Farming was not promising, so I hoped to find a job and take care of her. What was the result of my mother's many years of suffering? She became hypertensive. No surprise to me. She had worked too hard. From around the age of forty-seven, her health began to fail. I felt so bad as I watched her suffer. I felt this ache deep inside my bones. I hoped day after day that life would improve and that somehow things would get better, but as the days wore on, there was no good change.

At certain times, it is difficult to force things to happen in the way you want. If a human being could force things to happen, then 1997 was my year. The phrase "go to university" was by then part of my consciousness and my unconsciousness. I believe I was uttering this phrase even in my sleep. If the phrase "go to university" was a mantra for enlightenment, I should have been swimming in enlightened bliss at that time. It was like there were some noises in my head saying "go to university", "go to university."

With this phrase storming me minute by minute, hour by hour and day by day, I set off in November 1997 straight to seek registration in the university nearest to my hometown. That was the University of Dschang in the West Region of Cameroon. I had two relatives already studying there, so I met them in their apartment and told them I had come to register. The next day I went to the department of social sciences to seek admission. I wanted to read Sociology. The registrar told me admission was already closed, therefore I would not have a place. I went home to my relatives' apartment and told them the registrar informed me that admission was over and I did not have a chance. My relatives told me to put some money in an envelope and hand it to that man in the office, and he would submit. The next day I put 2000 FCFA, which was about $4, in an envelope and went to the office. I handed the envelope together with my documents to the registrar. He took the envelope and my documents and smiled broadly. He looked at my documents and saw I came from Santa. He asked, "Do you know Achidi Achu"? (He was a prominent politician and one time Prime Minister of Cameroon). I answered, "Yes, he is from Santa, my hometown." He admitted me, matriculated 97L443, in the department of Sociology, Psychology and Philosophy, and my major was Sociology.

That is not all. Because I did not have money, after securing my place at the University, I went home to see how I could raise money and return to class. I stayed home and only returned around January 15. I got a tiny room for 5000 FCFA a month, which is about $10. The exams were to begin in a week, and I had no notes. I bought notes from one student who had two copies of all the notes in all the courses. However, the University of Dschang is a French speaking university, so the notes were in French, and at that time I was blank as far as French was concerned. The exams were already too close. I had to look for a student who was good in both French and English and pay him or her to translate the notes for me. The other students of English language origin laughed at me, because they were at the university since September, and they were not coping with the university system either. In any case, I had a kind of stubborn confidence in me that I would succeed. I was not at all afraid.

The exams for modern sociology were the coming week. As the notes had already been translated into English, I mastered them.

The next funny thing was that the morning of the exams, I came late. I entered the hall when all the students were busy writing. The students, especially the English-speaking ones, raised their eyebrows at me. They laughed again, probably thinking, what kind of a man is this? The professor gave me the question, and it was in French. By some magic, I understood it. I asked the professor if I still had enough time to answer it. He said something I heard as twenty minutes. Normally I would have considered twenty minutes very normal, because in the Anglophone system of education, we wrote our tests or small exams in thirty minutes or at most forty-five. I quickly drew lines on the answer sheet without a ruler. I filled two answer sheets in less than twenty minutes. Then I sat waiting to hand over my answer sheets. Instead, I heard the Professor announce we had one hour left. That was when I learned they give a lot of time to Francophones to write a simple test. I finally understood that they gave us two hours to write the test on that day. I was so shocked. I read over my work and corrected mistakes where I thought necessary. To the surprise of my Anglophone brothers and sisters, I passed that test and they failed. I continued there at the University of Dschang until April when I was completely broke. I had no money and no food; it was very difficult for me.

One day I was in my room. A classmate of mine came and told me he saw my name pasted on the notice board, with a note saying a visiting lecturer from the University of Yaounde asked to see me. I made the sign of the cross and doubted what for. I left my room immediately with the friend and went to the campus. I met the man delivering lectures. He said my uncle in the United States of America sent some money that he should give me. I took the envelope and saw 50 000 FCFA, which is about $100. I thanked the Professor and left. That was a miracle for me. Instantly my problems vanished, and I studied without any financial problems until July when we had holidays. I wrote to my uncle in the United States of America and thanked him for the wonderful gift. Without this money, I would have abandoned my studies before July. I wrote all the exams. But all along, it was not easy for the Anglophone students to pass most of the courses in one sitting. I passed some of the courses and returned in September to rewrite the courses I failed. Luckily, I did well in the courses I wrote in September. I had more than a 70% pass rate in all my courses, which qualified me for level two.

By October 1998, luck was no longer on my side. There was no uncle to give me another $100 to help me continue my studies for the second year. Therefore, I had to drop out of university. That was the fifth year after high school. I left and was at home again and in the farms working morning and evening. I kept on in the farms. Until one day in early April 1999 when I was in the farms, and my eyes suddenly went dark. As if I were blind. I had never felt that way before. Though it happened only for a few seconds, I felt sick. I could not continue to work. I marched home with my work tools. I fell sick and was diagnosed with malaria. I stayed in the hospital for treatment.

After a week, I went back to the farms. Then in May, I suddenly fell sick again. I went back to the hospital, and this time the lab results showed no malaria and no typhoid. I was constantly anaemic. This began as a joke, but I stayed under this condition from May 1999 to around the year 2004. My entire body was aching, my tongue was as dry as a desert, my legs were paining, and I had serious headaches. I could not read for more than five minutes at a time, for if I tried, tears would start running down my cheeks. When the rays of the sun touched me, it was as if I would collapse. The sun became my number one enemy. I left the house very early each morning, went and harvested pepper from my farm, and returned early enough – by 9 o'clock – before the sun arrested me. This unknown disease was making me mad. All medical checks at the hospital found nothing wrong with me.

One day at the Akum mission hospital, the doctor asked me to do an HIV test. I tried to tell him that for the past two years I had used preservatives. The doctor was a white man. He shouted, "No, no, go and do the test!" I was afraid. The idea of doing that test took me by surprise, so I told the doctor I would come back later. I gathered courage and returned after a few days for the test and fortunately, it was negative. Because it was negative, the doctor kept giving me antibiotics for many months, but I did not know what the medications were treating. When I was tired taking the antibiotics, I decided to go elsewhere and seek treatment. I went to St. Louis Hospital in Bamenda. The lab results took 25 000 FCFA ($50) from me, and the doctor said nothing much was found in the results. They prescribed drugs for me, which I bought. Spending so much money on that day flattened me. They told me to come back when I finished the drugs, but that would be impossible because I had finished all my money there on that day.

I was sleeping sometimes for up to eighteen or nineteen hours a day. It was like death. Nothing could wake me when I was in those deep sleeps. I could not stay up for more than four hours. One day, as I was very confused about the deep sleep all the time, I went to the hospital and complained to the officer on sit that I wanted to do the test for sleeping sickness. He told me, "Please go away. If it was sleeping sickness you would not be standing there speaking." I went home more confused and still not knowing what was wrong with me. My sleeps were full of dreams, from America to Cameroon, from west to east, from heaven to earth, from body to spirit and from spirit to body. It was as if I had become a spirit, a body of dreams, and no longer a human being with flesh.

First I experienced a financial catastrophe to enter university, then a health calamity. I stopped thinking of university. I thought only of recovering my health and becoming normal as I used to be. By the end of 1999, the hospital declared I was in good health, but that was their declaration and not how I felt in my body. I still felt very sick. I still had all the symptoms I had in May. I had pains and headache, and felt anaemic. My tongue was as dry as bread, and I was plagued by the sleep of death. How could I be in good health while feeling this way? With this confusion, I left for a traditional healer by the end of 1999. For the whole of the year 2000, I spent my time at the traditional doctor's clinic. My health improved, but I did not completely recover and did not feel normal as I used to be. Then in the year 2001, I left the healer's place and went back home and stayed there with the illness.

By September 2001, my uncle encouraged me to write the entrance examination so I could train as a teacher. But serious headaches kept me from reading. With a lot of reluctance, I went in for the examination. When the results came out, I was successful. I went in for the training and did my possible, though I could not read much. I finally graduated and became a teacher in July 2002. However, the government was not recruiting teachers. The private schools and mission schools would pay around 40 000 FCFA ($80) a month. With this amount of money, how could I rent a house in the city and live there? It meant I had to live in the slums, and I never chose to live in the slums. At that time, the government was recruiting few teachers on contract basis. The number recruited was far less than the number who had graduated. The salary for those contract teachers was about $120 a month and only payable in nine of the twelve months of the year. The government encouraged the unemployed teachers to be teaching voluntarily in government schools without salaries, so that if it was time to recruit contract teachers, those teaching as volunteers would be the first to be recruited. I strongly believed in this government promise and decided to stay in my village and did voluntary work there. I was teaching children in the government school in my village. The parents of the children were giving me a monthly income of 12 000 FCFA ($24) a month. I was in the school until the end of 2004.

In September 2003, the government launched a campaign to recruit three thousand contract teachers. In the whole country, there were probably more than thirty thousand unemployed teachers. We went for the interview, and the whole place was like ants. We were so many. Just by seeing the number of us for the job interview, there was no hope I would have a chance. Finally it was over, and there was no recruitment for me. At that time, I knew that the government had tricked us. The government just fooled us into teaching in its schools. Therefore, at the end of school year, I started thinking of leaving the village for the city.

The frustration was terrible. Life was unbearable. My mind started ringing a new bell. "The village is not for you, go away, go to the city." I prepared myself to leave and go to the city, maybe to Yaounde; the political capital of Cameroon, or to Douala, the economic capital, to find a teaching job there and no doubt live in the slums. The salary would be at most 40 000 FCFA ($80) a month. I would have to rent a room and feed and clothe myself. Then suddenly, from the blue, I was not to go to Yaounde nor Douala. I had to board Ethiopian Airlines, fly to Addis Ababa, then over the ocean and over India, and finally settle in an unknown land. I couldn't have fathomed such a thing, even in my wildest dreams.

2

Where did the idea to travel to China come from?

The circumstances of my life in the year 2004 did not permit me to think of going abroad. Earning just 12 000 FCFA a month and experiencing poor health, I could not think of leaving Cameroon for China. All my farming could not yield much to help me leave the country. I had in mind that with all the misery, leaving the country for greener pasture was a great idea, which I loved. But it would be a waste of thoughts, because I did not have the means. My misery was great. I had only one pair of shoes and barely any clothes, which are basic things for a human being. I was wearing certain short trousers every day. One day when I was at home, I heard my stepsister had come from Douala with clothes and was in the market selling them. I went to the market to see if I could get some of the clothes for myself. The clothes were second-hand and not expensive. I thought I might take some and pay later. Then I realized I had a dollar in my pocket. I left the house and walked to the market. I found the clothes dumped in a pile before my stepsister. They were terrible. I could not imagine how a person could buy things like that. However, I gave her $1 and picked up a pair of trousers and a shirt. When I arrived home, I saw the clothes were actually rotten. I feared diseases if I put them on, and I never wore those clothes.

One day in December 2003, I returned from the farm. I had worked hard that day and was very tired. I prepared dinner, ate and went to bed. At night, I had a certain dream.

In the dream was a message. The message was clear. I did not doubt what I heard. This was the message: "You have been admitted to a medical school abroad." I knew everything was possible, but I never took this dream seriously because of all my frustration and misery. Moreover, I knew that to study medicine at university one has to have read the sciences. I instead studied the arts in high school, and I did not see myself entering a medical university, and more so abroad. By all human calculations and judgment, everything pointed to no. It was just a dream, and it was not a true dream. But I did not forget the dream.

I had learnt a few herbs from my father, so as I worked in the farm, I also found time to harvest herbs. I frequently visited the forest to harvest herbs, dry them, then package and store them. I learnt about other herbs as I went around. I would treat myself with the herbs and gave them to others on demand. One day my stepbrother took some of the herbs when he was not feeling fine. He met a certain woman who was also sick and gave her part of the herbs. He told me that he heard a knock on his door at 5 o'clock in the morning and opened the door. The woman he gave the herbs to was facing him. At first he feared that maybe those herbs had caused some damage, and trouble was around. However, it was the contrary. The woman said, "Go and show me the doctor who gave you those herbs. When I took them my stomach pains that have tortured me for many years vanished automatically." My brother told me this, but I was still not convinced I was qualified to enter a medical school. I thought that I might be an herbalist, a native or traditional doctor, but never a medical doctor trained in a college of modern medicine.

14

By this time, a relative of mine whom we should call Mr. Thomson, who had lived together with me in the same house for some time, saw me gathering herbs. He was at the university, and before he left for class, he took some of the herbs from me. He later told me that whenever he had a cold, he would infuse some of those powdered herbs in water and drink. He said when he took the herbs like tea, his cold would disappear. Mr. Thomson later travelled to China to work as an acupuncturist (which he had learnt privately while studying at the university) and to learn Chinese medicine as a whole and make it a career.

Since Mr. Thomson left for China in September 2003, we were not in touch for a while. One day I thought it would be good to be in touch with him, but I did not know how. How could I get in touch with him? I had heard there was something called the internet where you can send letters to correspondents and they receive them immediately. However, in my hometown there was no computer and of course no internet. Very few people in my hometown had heard that word "internet", so if you pronounced that word, most people would look at you with a blank stare. When I dropped out of the University of Dschang, I had a friend. I had met him, and he told me he was learning the computer. Therefore, I thought that if somebody was learning the computer, he should know about this magic called the internet. I took a taxi from my hometown of Santa to meet him in Bamenda (the capital of the North West Region of Cameroon). The distance is about thirty kilometres. I met him, and at that time, he was studying peace studies at a private university. I told him my mission, "I want to send greetings to my relative in China. Can you help me send an email to him?" He agreed that there was no problem in that. I dictated the mail to him, and he typed it and saved it in a USB key so that when we arrived at the net bar, he could just send it.

We went to the net bar, and I paid $1 for an hour. For the first fifteen minutes, it was terrible. The computers were archaic, and the internet line was too slow. It took us about twenty minutes to get into his inbox. I gave him the email address of my relative, and he sent the email through his own email, for I did not yet have one. This was around August 2004. I returned to my friend after a week. We checked his mail, and the reply was there. Mr. Thomson was very positive. He was very happy I had written to him. He asked a question that took me by surprise: "Would you like to come to China and study Chinese medicine?" This question was a big surprise to me. I suddenly remembered the dream of 2003. Yes, that I should go abroad and enter a medical university. I asked my friend what answer Mr. Thomson expected from me except a big "yes." This was the opportunity to leave, for the level of frustration was already so high. I did not have any other choice before me. If I started thinking, where I would have money to undertake that mission, more complications would set in, so I told my friend to reply to the email and answer "Yes."

On that same day, I arranged with my friend to come back so he could teach me how to open the computer and send emails too. I returned, and the first class was at the campus of his university. First, he taught me how to turn on the computer, followed by how to download and save data in both the internal and external drives of the computer. I took down notes on how to do the things he taught me. I think I was fast in learning. After that, we went to the net bar, and he taught me how to sign in using my username and password. I can remember the first days learning this. It was as if I should never understand the computer. The computer screen standing before me was like the dashboard of a plane. I did not know where to begin and end. There was too much information, and I did not know which to focus on. It was as if I should never understand it. I just took down a few notes, and in the future when facing the screen, I had to look for key words like "sign in", "check mail", "inbox", and "sign out". I would ignore the rest, otherwise confusion would set in. I later started searching by Google and Yahoo search engines. I found it very exciting. I would type something I wanted to know. Then information about things I had thought difficult to have knowledge about flashed before me. How exciting. We see how life had changed within a short time. The computer and the internet, at first a miracle, within a few years became our daily friend. From that time onwards, I could operate the computer and the internet by myself. Therefore, I kept in touch with Mr. Thomson without the aid of my friend.

By this time, my friend who had just earned his degree in peace studies also wrote to Mr. Thomson, asking him for help to go to China and study Chinese medicine as well. Mr. Thomson agreed to find him a place in the university and to help him and me get a visa. Mr. Thomson was my relative and also my friend. Because my friend did not know Mr. Thomson, he agreed to pay 200 000 FCFA ($400) to Mr. Thomson when he received his visa. For me, Mr. Thomson's services were gratis. With everything well set, from September 2004, my friend and I were on the way to the Chinese consulate to process our visas to China. Yes, on the way for the Visa. My friend was as poor as I was, and he had more troubles even perhaps than I. We never thought how we would travel to China. On foot, by car, by ship or by plane. We never answered these questions, and how we would get to China was the unanswered mystery.

3

Visa process at the Chinese consulate in Douala in Cameroon

My friend and I travelled to the Chinese consulate in Douala to see if we could get visas to travel to China. It was not easy. We were two confused and frustrated souls, yet we were ready to board a plane and go abroad. Among almost all the youths in Cameroon, the most spoken word is "abroad." My uncle, brother, sister, relative, uncle's friend or brother's friend is in this or that country. They will help me go abroad. That is it. They do not know what this or that person is doing abroad but only that he will help me go abroad. They mention these relatives are in Europe, America and Canada. They never mention African countries, for it might be a curse to leave from an African country and enter another African country. The European countries like France, Italy, Spain, England, and Germany are on the list. America and Canada are very famous on the list. America is the most famous.

Relatives leave these countries and come home in the dry season, between November and March, for weddings and celebrations. If they came in the rainy season, from March to October, the heavy rains would hinder all the grandiose outdoor activities. Their presence in town is a period the locals never forget. When those relatives are around, money flows around like leaves of trees. In short, the air is different. The visiting relatives pump and spread money around. In America and Europe there are trees where money is harvested, but unfortunately our soils are too barren for that kind of tree. What a curse! We Africans are not lucky.

For these people from America and Europe, coins do not exist, even old bank notes do not exist, and everything in the name of money is bright new bank notes. We see these people almost like beings from other worlds, like super humans. Most of them wear black suits and black hats, but some of them still dress normal. Even if they dress normal, just with a T-shirt and a pair of trousers and tennis shoes, news still goes around and everyone still knows them. When they are around, word spreads like wildfire. Everywhere they pass, fingers point at them and people say, "He is from America." These people drive very big cars and carry an air of importance. Most of them do not sleep in the houses they stayed in before they went abroad. They sleep in big hotels and return in the morning for festivities. If you are a lucky young girl, one of these great men may soon extend a hand to you and say, "I would like you to be my wife." We who were living in the country saw how these brothers and sisters from faraway lands came home and acted. We wanted to be like them. Their lives were wonderful lives that we all envied. We wanted their kind of living.

My friend and I loved this kind of good life too. We wanted to go to America and Europe too, but because we didn't know how to go about that, we humbly accepted the offer of Mr. Thomson to help us travel to China. For my friend and me, this was a must-grab opportunity. Mr. Thomson, who had left just a year ago, before my very eyes, was asking me to come and meet him there in China. Somebody who had lived in the same house with me and ate in the same bowl with me was asking me to come and meet him. Even the hurricane Sandy could not have stopped me from going to China. Nothing could change my course. By 2004, China was already on the list for Africans aiming to go abroad. With the doors of Europe and America closed on me, the door of China was widely opened and I had to walk through it.

With all my determination, I decided to travel to Douala for my visa to travel to China. I did not have the transport to go to Douala. I needed about 15 000 FCFA ($30) for the trip. It had already been a year since my mother started to lose her sight. She had a cataract in her eye, and I had to take her to the hospital to get it removed. That would cost about 50 000 FCFA ($100). This was urgent as the distance she could see was shortening almost weekly. I could not sit and see her lose her sight. By some luck, I succeeded in raising the money, went with her to the hospital, and the cataract was taken care of. The operation was very successful. It has now been seven years, and her sight is very stable.

After my mother's treatment, I was lucky enough to raise some money again for the trip to the Chinese consulate. My friend and I went straight to the Chinese consulate in Douala and met the assistant consular officer. He could only speak Chinese and French. My friend and I were Anglophone. The officer was asking us questions in French. Even with the little we understood, we were unable to reply. I tried desperately to explain things to the man, but my friend sat cool and never said a word. We had brought our school certificates and the admission letters Mr. Thomson had sent from China. The officer told us we should ask Mr. Thomson to fax the same documents he had sent to us to him at the consulate. We wrote to Mr. Thomson, and he faxed the documents. We returned to the Consulate in about a week's time. This was still in September 2004.

We arrived there with high hopes. Hopeful as we were, we did not really know what it would take to get a visa. Yet we thought everything was possible. However, we later realized it was not easy. First, we were going to study in China for an indefinite length of time. Therefore, we had to show some proof of financial backing, how we were to live and pay our tuition in China without major problems. This meant that a bank statement was necessary, and we had to undergo an elaborate medical test to be sure we had no dangerous or chronic disease. Therefore, without bank statements showing our financial capabilities and a medical certificate, the officer rejected our documents. When we heard of the medical certificate, we thought we could go to any public hospital and pick one for about 2 500 FCFA ($5). In Cameroon when you need a medical certificate, you just go to the hospital and get one for that amount. I had had many a medical certificate, but no doctor ever examined me before issuing it.

Instead, the man gave us an address of a Chinese hospital, to go there and do the medical examinations. We thought it might cost each person about $10 or $15 dollars. To our surprise, the total amounted to about 100 000 FCFA ($200). We stood there confused and not knowing what to do. We had very little money. We pleaded with the chief doctor. He scrapped some of the tests, and everything was then totalling 50 000 FCFA ($100). The doctor took our blood samples, and we paid the little money we had on the spot. I went my way, my friend also went his, both of us with one thing in mind: "How to get the money to pay for the medical examination." One way was to ask for support from relatives. My friend was the last in his family. Most of his elder brothers are priests in the Catholic Church. They were serving the lord and had no money to help him. I saw my friend suffered for years in great misery. He lacked money to pay his school fees and buy food. His brothers had only the word of god to give him. He told me his elder brothers told him that his destiny was the priesthood and that all his suffering was because he never accepted to join the priesthood. Maybe this was not a joke, for he ended up as a pastor in his own church created by the lord. We never gave up. My little sister and some relatives aided me with the money, and my friend raised his own part of the money in his own way.

We went and paid the remaining money and got the test results. The HIV test, which was the most important, was negative for both of us. Nevertheless, the other tests indicated some minor problems that had to be treated. The doctor told us to get treatment for those problems before a medical certificate could be issued. We asked how much this treatment would cost. The doctor said each of us needed to pay 100 000 FCFA ($200). For my friend and me, that money was too much. We did not know how to raise this kind of money again. We pleaded to the doctor that we needed the medical certificates urgently and that we would treat ourselves elsewhere. The doctor was highly understandable and gave us the medical certificate. My lab result showed traces of chlamydia, for which I later met a friend, a naturopath, and took herbal concoctions to treat myself. I had no idea what my friend did with the typhoid fever that showed in his lab results. We were very busy fighting to get our visas. I never asked him what happened with his typhoid, and as far as I remember, I never heard him ask me anything about my own illness.

After we had the medical certificates, we then needed bank statements to complete our documents. This bank statement must contain enough money in it, showing that we could pay for our studies and cover all our expenses in China. My friend and I had never had bank accounts. This was no easy task. Nevertheless, as soon as we separated, luck fell on my friend. His days were full of sunshine and bright weather while my days were full of dark clouds. My friend quickly found a relative who blessed him with a bank statement to go for his visa. That was the last document we needed, so his file was complete. With a broad smile and unspeakable speed, he was there at the Chinese consulate. He deposited his documents, and his visa was granted in November 2004 and was valid until February 2005. Therefore, by all means, the task before him was to enter China before the expiration date in February.

I had to fight to get my own bank statement. This was no easy task. I tried so hard but to no avail. Though I never had a bank account, I was confident I would find someone to bless me with a statement. I contacted people, but nobody could help. I went from person to person. All I heard was, "No way." I contacted people until I did not know where to turn. Had it been I knew the house of Satan, I might have gone there too to ask for a bank statement. Then one day I remembered a certain man for whom I had great respect. He could be sixty years old. This very man once helped me through a very serious problem. I asked myself why I had not thought of him before. I went and met him at his home. I told him my problem. "I want a bank statement to go and get my visa to China." The man replied that it was no problem. He said my problem was as simple as making a cup of tea. That I should go and ready myself to travel to Douala in a day or two. He said he needed just one thing from me, and that was 20 000 FCFA ($40). I did not have the money with me. I left and did all things possible to get the money, and I gave it to him the next day. Funny things started to happen. It was not long before I realized this man had duped me. He gave me only promises each time I met him, until I got tired and left. This man, the angel who once saved me from a serious problem, was then the devil who killed me. At a time when money was so hard for me, a man I trusted duped $40 from me in broad daylight.

This was a bitter pill for me to swallow. It was already November, and I had not yet come up with this bank statement. I contacted the manager of a small bank in my hometown to help me with a bank statement in his own name. He agreed. There was no delay. I was happy. I was close to having what I most wanted. Miracles were already happening, I thought. The manager went to his computer and after clicking a few times, a sheet of paper came out of the machine standing by the computer. He gave it to me, and I thanked him. I was extremely happy. I did not read the document. From my hometown, I went to Bamenda. From there, I had to continue to Douala and go straight to the Chinese consulate for the visa. Just as I was about to travel, I thought it wise for me to read what was written on the bank statement. I read it, and I was satisfied, until I saw the figures. The amount of money mentioned was 300 000 FCFA ($600). That amount was way too small. I would be a fool to carry that statement to the consulate. The money on the statement could not even pay my flight, let alone my fees and rents. It was a good for nothing bank statement. Did the bank manager know this? I had told him why I wanted the statement.

In any case, I suspended my trip. It was already early December. I returned to my hometown, not knowing the next person to contact. It was now time for prayer and meditation. All the saints in the Catholic church suffered in my hands. I am sure those saints could not rest. I was launching prayers second by second, minute by minute, hour by hour and day by day. If we could see thoughts and words with the physical eyes, I am sure my thoughts and prayer words were more abundant than dust particles. I rang the alarm bell so hard with prayers and meditations. Saint Jude, Saint Anthony of Padua, the rosary, and the holy mother of god were on the list. No need mentioning the lord Jesus Christ; he could not fail to be on the list. No doubt, I had changed my church in August, just a few months before, from the Presbyterian (which does not believe in the saints) to the Catholic church. I kept hammering prayers for the whole month of December until somehow I started seeing bank statements in my dreams. Bank statement became my most spoken word. If not verbally, I was intuitively attuning to it. If bank statement was a mantra for enlightenment, I would have been enlightened that same year.

Then one day around the 12th of December, I thought of a friend who was a young businessperson. I went and asked him to help me with a bank statement. He agreed and gave me one. I glanced over the figures in it. Not so much money, but far better than in the statement I'd received from the bank manager. I travelled with it, and on the 15th of December 2004, I was at the Chinese consulate in Douala. I presented my file, but the assistant counsellor officer complained that schools began in September, and it was already December. He said it was not possible to give me a visa. I do not know what spoke to him in the end, whether it was my beseeching eyes, my bewildered being, my numerous pleas, all of the above or something else. But he finally agreed to give me a visa. They told me to come with 45 000 FCFA ($90) the next week and get my visa. This was wonderful news for me, but this money of $90 was not an easy task.

My little sister, a private teacher in Yaounde earning 40 000 FCFA ($80) a month, contributed most of the money. I went to the Chinese consulate on the appointed day, paid the money and received my passport with my visa in it. An "X" visa, issued 22 December 2004 and valid until 22 March 2005. Wonderful emotions filled me. Words could not express my feelings on that day. I felt great bliss. I felt a heavy load lifted off my shoulders. I looked at the stamped visa on my passport. It was wonderful. I, earning 12 000 FCFA ($24) a month, was holding a visa to China in my hands. This was unbelievable. The American dream was already working inside me in a land, far, far away from America. How could this happen? The American dream became the world's dream. My own personal dream of December 2003, about being admitted to a medical university abroad, was coming true.

4

How could I raise 700 000 francs (1400 dollars) to buy my ticket?

As I had the visa in hand, I called one of my little sisters and some of my relatives and informed them I had the visa. They did not take it lightly. There was great joy. I went home to await my cousin with whom I had stayed all along in Douala during the visa process. When she returned home, I told her the surprise news: "Visa in hand." It was wonderful. She said an "X" visa was not the easy type to have. "X" means it is a student visa for an indefinite stay as compared to an "F" (business) visa or an "L" (tourist) visa. We rejoiced in this miracle. I also informed Mr. Thomson that I had the visa already, and he expressed great joy and promised he would send my flight ticket.

From Douala, I returned to my hometown in Santa in north-western Cameroon. I stayed home. I patiently waited for my flight ticket. If by any chance Mr. Thomson did not send it as promised, I had to be hoping for other avenues. While waiting for divine grace to do its work, I thought it was time for me to do some charity work. Therefore, I went back to the school in my village where I had been teaching for two years for almost nothing as a salary. They had given me 12 000 FCFA ($24) a month. I decided to continue the charity work there in January and February, leaving the $24 a month to my parents.

Things were not easy. There were many obstacles. The days wore by, and I never had means to buy the flight ticket. December passed, and I did not have this money. January came and went, no ticket; February came and went, no money. March 2005 came, and I did not have this ticket. Everything was so silent about my ticket. Nothing was working for me. It was as if the gods too had forgotten about me. My visa indicated, "Enter before March 22nd 2005." It was already early March. What could I do to enter China before March 22? I was confused. It was urgent and necessary that I enter China. My misery was unbearable. I did all the prayers and meditations a human being could do when facing a situation. I did novenas after novenas to the saints. I called on the angels, the saints and my ancestors and put my problem to them. I had been launching these prayers since January, and by March I started having ecstatic dreams and visions. In the dreams and visions, I was already in China, and it was a wonderful life. I felt the bliss only to realize later it was a dream. I dreamt that all difficulties were already resolved and I was right there in China. These dreams were happening frequently until I told myself that these dreams meant my spirit was already in China, and if the spirit was there, it meant I was there. I told myself that if my spirit was already there, it meant that something would eventually happen to move my body to join its spirit counterpart in China. I strongly believed it like this, and that eventually happened.

I had written to my uncle in the United States of America in January and told him I had my visa to China and needed help to buy the ticket. I had not heard the reply, so I wrote again in February reminding – imploring – him to assist me for my flight ticket. It was already early March, and I had not yet heard anything. Around the 10th of March – just ten days before the invalidity of my visa –, I almost gave up. With just ten days remaining, what could happen? In life one never knows. A surprise happened on March 15. My cousin in Douala gave me a phone call. She said my uncle in the United States sent 450 000 FCFA ($900) to help me buy my flight to China. When I heard this news, I could not express my feelings in words. I was extremely happy. I felt a kind of bliss I had never felt. I felt as if something had lifted me from the ground and I was floating. I felt so light, almost like a feather. It was as if the force of gravity had no effect on me.

My mind started reflecting what I should do to raise more money and add to that which my uncle sent. The way I was thinking, I could not express in words. My thoughts were as if what I was thinking was there in front of me. It was as if I suddenly developed the IQ of Bill Clinton. With these swift thoughts telling me where to go and get money, I rushed to one relative of mine and asked him to lend me money. He lent me 190 000 FCFA ($380), and I had to pay back with interest. I rushed to another relative who also lent me 35 000 FCFA ($70). Another uncle sent me $40. So instantly on that day I was able to raise $490. Adding this sum to that which my uncle had sent from the United States, it was already enough to pay my flight. I put all the money I borrowed in a bundle and not in a purse. I went to my uncle's room, opened a book, and hid the money inside. The money was quietly lying there.

I planned to leave my hometown in the next two days and travel to Douala, from where I would eventually fly. The day finally arrived when I had to leave my hometown. It was March 17. I went to the bookshelf where I had hid the money. I pulled out the textbook, opened it and took out the money. What a shock! The money was still in the bundle as I had put it, however one funny thing had happened. In a zigzag way, some invisible thing had cut all the edges of the money in the bundle. Therefore, I had hid the money from thieves and given it to invisible enemies. Who were they? Who were the actors of this malicious work? Were they visible or invisible enemies? How would I buy the ticket with money half eaten? Who wanted to see me fail? One thing was clear; we would say it was the handwork of rats or cockroaches. Even if they were rats and cockroaches, in Africa it was a bad sign. A sign that something was wrong somewhere. A sign of enemies approaching, a danger sign, a bad omen. I slowly opened my bundle and noticed that the enemies ate the money but did not reach the bank note figures. The invisible enemies had left the figures of that money intact. Here in Cameroon, if something eats up the figures of a bank note, the money is useless because nobody will accept it. In Africa, bank notes that have lost any of their figures are a taboo. People withdraw as if it is poison when they set eyes on such bank notes. If this money had lost any of its figures, I would not have travelled and would still have had to pay the money back to the people who lent it to me.

In any case, the money was still usable, so I had to move on. I said goodbye to my mother and a few other people. Many things were still uncertain. I had only the exact money to buy the flight. There was nothing for fees, no pocket money, and nothing for lodging. For these reasons, I thought it unwise to go around announcing I was going abroad, so there were no elaborate celebrations. If a few people were aware, that was enough.

My friend, who had obtained his visa in November failed to travel. He lacked money to pay his ticket. Even if he had money to pay the ticket, he was afraid of so many things. He had heard there were no jobs in China, and so he was afraid to frustrate himself. Many friends told him that others had returned from China because they found no jobs. In addition, he did not have his fees to study in the medical school. Therefore, he was very afraid, and his visa expired. I told him that even if it was a war, I would go to China to fight, and never did I know what I was saying, for my stay in China was truly a war, a fight that would not end. My friend also failed to pay Mr. Thomson the money he agreed to pay him for helping him get his visa. One day I went and met my friend's elder brother who was a priest. I told him that Mr. Thomson wanted his money. That he should pay the money 200 000 FCFA ($400). He replied, "Mr. Thomson wants money when nothing yet has worked. There is no money." I stood there confused. The agreement was that his brother gets a visa. Whether he travelled or not, it was not Mr. Thomson's problem. I saw how a priest was dishonest in the open. My friend failed to travel, and by that response it meant his elder brother, a priest, supported his idea not to pay the money. My friend failed to travel, but the divine was gradually settling in him. He joined a charismatic prayer group in the Catholic church, and when he prayed with others, miracles happened. When he prayed, a breeze would blow among the members of the group, and many other things would happen. The bishop was conscious of these curiosities and anxious about my friend, so he suspended him from praying in the group. During this time of suspension, a revelation came to my friend that the lord wanted him to open his own church, which he did. Until this day, he is a pastor in his own church.

I arrived in Douala on March 17 and handed the money I brought to my cousin. She put all the money together and bought my ticket. I saw the ticket and the flight itinerary. It was great seeing all these wonderful things. These were good things, and I was pleased to see them happening. I stayed in my cousin's house for three days. The flight was on Sunday, 21 March 2005 at 3:30 pm, on Ethiopian Airlines. That Sunday finally came. I was happy. Everyone was happy. It was my cousin and her friend, and my little sister. We all got ready and got into my cousin's car. We took off in the direction of the Douala airport. I started feeling some strange thoughts on the way. I started having many doubts about everything. Things came to my mind like, how would I survive in China? Questions came to my mind like, I was going to meet Mr. Thomson in China, and all along, he had not honoured most of his promises to me, so how would I cope?

First of all Mr. Thomson had promised to help me financially to get my visa, which he never did. Second, he promised to send my flight ticket, which he never did. I wondered, if he had failed twice in promises to me, could I actually trust him? What would happen when I entered China? Doubts and confusion were ringing in my mind on the way to the airport. In addition, on the day I was travelling Mr. Thomson was not in China but in Europe. My cousin called Mr. Thomson and asked him, now that he was in Europe, what would happen when I arrived in China. He replied that the school authorities would pick me up at the Beijing international airport. Oh I thought, the wind becomes a storm, raindrops become a heavy downpour. Confusion, worries and doubts transformed into fear in less than one minute. When going for the visa, I made it clear to Mr. Thomson that I had no money, and we agreed I should stay at home with him and only attend school when I had money. Now the school would be picking me up at the airport? They were taking me to Mr. Thomson's house? The answer was no! They were taking me to school. Then they would ask for my tuition, lodging, bills and all kinds of things.

I thought of my friend who became a pastor. He had a clear vision of China and refused to travel. I was crazy. I was on the way to the airport before realizing I was about to fall in the waterloo pit. I was standing at the edge of the pit that brought down Napoleon Bonaparte. I coughed and explained to my cousin my doubts. Mr. Thomson was in Europe. The school was picking me up. I had no fees. How would all that work? She was not happy with these questions and replied, "Stop expressing doubt when people are struggling that you go abroad." However, that did not quell my doubts.

She asked if I had my yellow fever vaccination card. I said, "I have my passport and visa. I do not know what you are talking about." She got so angry and asked me again, "How can you go abroad without a vaccination card? That is enough to stop you from travelling!" Her friend who was sitting by her calmed her down said she would try to get that yellow fever vaccination card for me at the airport. For me, I knew I passed the medical test and had my visa. That was all I knew, and nobody ever told me about a certain vaccination card. When we arrived at the airport, my cousin left us for a few minutes. She returned with a vaccination card for me, and it indicated I had had the yellow fever vaccination.

While we were at the airport, fear had not left me. I had only about 90 000 FCFA ($180) to carry with me as I travelled. I was thinking that rather than be frustrated in China, I would cancel my flight and use the money to start a small business. The school was receiving me at the airport and taking me to school. The way I judged the situation, I would not have my fees. I had no guarantee that Mr. Thomson would be able to support me financially. But I knew my cousin would oppose any further doubts about my travel. I wanted to talk to Mr. Thomson. Therefore, in order to avoid her, I begged her phone and went to a corner of the airport. I hid there where my cousin and her friend and my sister could not see me. I dialled Mr. Thomson's number in Europe and asked, "Please, you say the school will pick me up at the airport. I have no money for fees or lodging. How will this work out?"

He replied, "Please follow them and go to school. They will lead you into your apartment. Tell them all problems will be resolved on my return." With this phone call, fear disappeared from my spirit. I was confident. In an instant, a broad smile overtook my face. It was like the sun rose on my forehead. My mind was then fully prepared for China. I bid farewell to my cousin, her friend and my sister. Thanks be to god. What we never thought of finally happened.

5

A medical student at the Taiyuan University of Traditional Chinese Medicine

Taiyuan is the capital of Shanxi Province in China, and the medical school where I was to study is there. The foreign student department sent James (one of the staff) to receive me at the Beijing international airport. Our Ethiopian Airlines flight left Douala on Sunday, March 21, 2005 at 3:30 pm. My visa was valid until the next day, March 22. Because it was Ethiopian Airlines, we stopped over in Addis Ababa for about two hours. We took off and stopped over again in India for less than an hour. We took off and arrived in Beijing on Monday at 6:30 pm. This was already March 22, and I had just up until midnight for my visa to remain valid. I had never travelled before and was afraid. Because my visa had just a few hours of life left, I feared disaster. As I passed through various checkpoints, I imagined terrible things happening to me with an expired visa in hand. I regained my confidence as I passed through several checkpoints without interruption. Then I had my luggage with me. I helped another black woman who was carrying a big bag with difficulty as she carried her baby as well.

At the exit of the airport, I spotted my name held by James, a young staff of the Taiyuan medical college. I went straight to him and greeted him. He understood at once and asked if the name he was holding was mine. I agreed, and we got into a taxi at once and headed straight to the train station. He had bought our train tickets already to travel back to Taiyuan that same evening. At the train station, it was windy and a bit cold because it was spring. Although I was wearing a short sleeved shirt, I still felt a bit comfortable. James asked me, "Are you cold"? I said, "No, I am ok."

We boarded the train and James showed me my bed. He also went to his bed. There the long journey to Taiyuan began at 8 pm that same evening of my arrival in China. We travelled all night and arrived in Taiyuan city the next day. We took a taxi to school and James showed me to my room. It was on the fourth floor. It was an air conditioned single room and had a toilette and shower. It also had an outside kitchen for all the foreign students. There was a nice bed and a TV set. I was pleased with everything. The school authorities were so good to me. Studies had begun since September. Therefore, I began my own classes in the second semester. The school wanted me to catch up, so they said they would arrange extra classes for me during the summer holiday to meet up with the work of the first semester and move on to year two together with the others. I began to attend regular classes with the school. I loved the classes. I had that good feeling within that I could be a doctor, and then I would return to Africa and help my people. I studied herbology, diagnostics, basic theory of traditional Chinese medicine and other courses. With my long interest in herbs, I found herbology very interesting. However, as a first time learner of Chinese medicine, the concepts were entirely new to me. I quickly realized that Chinese medicine was so developed and with in-depth study could make one an outstanding doctor.

My studies were going on well. I quickly picked up the basic theories of traditional Chinese medicine. I was a stranger to Chinese medicine yet felt I picked up knowledge I had known before. Things were smooth. I never found the basic theories and general concepts of traditional Chinese medicine strange. My studies were going on well, but I had no idea where I would find money to pay my fees. Entering China with just 90 000 FCFA ($180) in my pocket was something very difficult.

The school authorities had asked me about paying my tuition and lodging. Mr. Thomson had promised that on his return from Europe that situation would be resolved. Therefore, the school was very satisfied with me. They did the best they could to see that I studied well and lived without any problems as a student of the school. In the first week of April 2005, Mr. Thomson returned from Europe. I was very happy to learn that he returned, for I knew he was my hope. He would assist me in my problems. Maybe I would have peace for the first time since I graduated from high school eleven years ago. However, this hope never materialized. It did not take me long to notice that the air was to be different. Things would not be as smooth as I had hoped. Another struggle was brewing. There would be no peace. Mr. Thomson told me nothing serious on his return. He would only say, "We will see how your tuition can be paid." He could not sit face to face with me, for even one minute. This was because he knew that if we did, I would start asking questions about my fees and lodging. These were things he never wanted to hear. Asking questions about money, fees and lodging was like giving holy water to the devil to drink. Therefore, we only met or sat where others were present. That saved him the hell of me asking inappropriate questions.

For the first two months, Mr. Thomson was giving me 50 Chinese Yuan ($7) for my food. Thank god food in Taiyuan city was cheap. During my second month in China, I began teaching one private weekend class, and I started earning a little money to feed myself. Days were passing, and gradually it became clear that Mr. Thomson did not have much to offer me. Things took a different direction. Mr. Thomson never had money but said he had spirituality to offer. He became a preacher of spiritual techniques to me. He became "my guru, my spiritual teacher." And would fill my ears with things such as: "You lack money or anything else because you lack the spiritual technique to materialize these things into your life. Just by entering China, you have gone far, and you can resolve the rest of the issues."

I did not personally reject this philosophy of being able to meditate and pray to bring goodness to life, but we have to respect our promises to our fellow human beings. I think many things determine whether people have money and get their problems solved. There are highly developed spiritual men and women in the world, but we see them suffer like every other human being. They have diseases, they are poor, depressed and the list is long. On the other hand, there are people who are extraordinarily rich who do not pray and some who do not even believe in meditation or the existence of god. I think that meditation and a good and poor life are complicated topics that we have to handle wisely. Before travelling to China, I was meditating and I still did while there, but I rejected the idea that I could lack the money to resolve my problems because I had a low level of spiritual development. I meditated seriously to resolve my problems daily and knew that by strong will, everything was possible, that was all.

June and July finally came, and there was no money. My fees and lodging were still pending. Nothing was yet paid. However, I wrote all my exams and did well in them. I passed all the courses I studied, and only how to finance my studies held me back. The school wanted money from me. Mr. Thomson gave me 2500 Yuan ($350), but it was not enough compared to what I owed the school. This sum could not quell the anger of the school. It was already early August, and September would soon come. In September, the new school year would begin, and the school would not let me into class still owing.

During this summer holiday of 2005, I met my first girlfriend in China. She was called Na. She fought hard and went into schools to help me find a job. She and I would take our bikes and go round the entire city looking for work, but it was not easy to find. All our efforts were dead ends. As a new person in China, if you are not a white, you will go through many obstacles before you have a job. You have to make many attempts. Each time you fall, you get up and make a new attempt. One day you pick up one job, and then the next and the next. And there you go, life starts going smoothly. However, for me, the pressure was too high. There was no time to spare. The school wanted money from me. I had to pay this money or else trouble would come.

One day a school called me up to come in and have my first trial class. Yes, this was a demonstration class to last for three hours. I was there as promised. The boss brought in the students. They knew my nationality as American because for those of us from Africa, we had to lie to get work. If known to be an African, especially as a newcomer, it would be hard to find work. I began the class, and I saw the students and the Chinese teachers and parents fidgeting. They could have been thinking, "What kind of American is that with that kind of accent?" I panicked and thought, "I have lost another job opportunity. Where will I get my fees?" The class was still going on when I heard a student sitting right in front of me

41

repeating the phrase "one hundred" and laughing. That was because I pronounced "hundred" with a strong "u" sound as we normally pronounce it in Africa. That depressed me. This class lasted three hours, and I thanked god it was finally over. The boss also seemed happy the class ended. I heard him apologizing to the parents about how they thought I was truly an American.

The boss took me to a nearby restaurant, gave me a plate of food, and vanished. It was later that I understood that normally he should have paid me for the three hours of work that morning. After that day, from time to time, he sent me messages expressing the hope that I might still work with him in the future. I did not know if he was serious or if he felt guilty, as he did not pay me for the work and abandoned me with low-grade food in that restaurant. Normally the parents of the children paid for the three-hour class. I did the work, and he kept all the money. However, an army never runs away from war. I learnt quickly from that what it took to teach English in China. I learnt how to pronounce words not as we do in Africa. I bought books in phonetics, followed BBC (British Broadcasting Corporation), VOA (Voice of America) and other news channels. After that, I had enough work. I had more work until I lacked time to take on new jobs.

But until then, I kept losing opportunities for work. Nothing was certain. September came, and my fees were not there. The school called Mr. Thomson to come, to all sit down together to see about the problem. He did not turn up. I was then a burden to the school. I told him that the school might want him to sign an agreement that I would pay the money later. He replied, "I am not signing anything." Then I told him that the school wanted him to come and sit down so we could talk. He replied harshly, "Here where I am sitting like this, I do not have one Yuan in my pocket to take a taxi." I told myself that if it had reached a level where Mr. Thomson lacked even one Yuan, then it was bad news for me.

A thousand questions came to my mind. Mr. Thomson fails me up to the level where he refuses to just sit and talk with the school. Then why did he agree even to the last minute that I come to China? I was really confused and I could not answer this question. Then after a few days, Mr. Thomson showed up at the school, but it was already late. The school lacked confidence in him, so they could not allow me to keep on with my studies. They had to let me go. At this point Mr. Thomson had negotiated a job for me through somebody so that I could leave the school, go to another city and work. The school let me go with the student visa with the hope that I would return, pay my fees from my job earnings, and continue in school. However, students are not supposed to work, so this was a risk, and more so because I was going to another city. This was thus risky for the school and for me too. Yet the next step was nevertheless for me to set off for work.

6

Teacher at number 1 middle school in Xian Yuan

Through a man called Michael, Mr. Thomson found me this job to teach English at number 1 middle school in Xiang Yuan. Xiang Yuan is a small district in Shanxi Province. Two of us had this job, both blacks. The school sent Mr. Wang Wen Xue, an English teacher, to Taiyuan to come and bring us to the school to sign the contract. When Mr. Wang came, he met Michael who introduced me saying, "This is Tardif from Holland." For this reason, throughout my stay at number 1 middle school, they knew me as a person who came from Holland. We went with Mr. Wang to Xiang Yuan and signed the contract for four months, from September 2005 through January 2006. If this job could go on for four months without problems, then it would go a long way to pay what I owed the medical school, though it could not pay it all. After signing the contract, we returned to Taiyuan to prepare ourselves to go for the job. Back in Taiyuan, the other foreign teacher who went and signed the contract with me refused to go for the job. However, for me, I had no option. I had to go for this work. Maybe he had other options from where he could solve his own problems, but for me I had no other solution to my problems.

On the day of my departure, the school sent Mr. Wang with a car to come and pick me up. Mr. Wang, the driver and I set off for Xiang Yuan. "Tardif from Holland" finally arrived at number 1 middle school in Xiang Yuan as the first foreign teacher the school and the district had ever had. To the Chinese, Africa was a place to build infrastructure, to create business, exploit oil and make money. It was not a place popular for English teachers. Therefore, it was not surprising that my nationality was not an African one. The Chinese are so curious to learn about the world, but Africa does not actually feature on their list. They are very much interested in learning about American and European culture but have no interest whatsoever in learning about African culture. If you are an African who can quickly twist your tongue to sound American or British, all the better for you. If you have a very strong accent that will not change, count on luck to find a job or else frustration and depression will sweep you away.

The journey to Xiang Yuan was good. Mr. Wang took me to my room. It was a clean room, and it had an outside toilette and shower. I had nothing to complain about. No matter the conditions, I was frustrated and just wanted a job and money. The same evening of my arrival, the principal of the school gave a welcome party for me. All the teachers were present in a long and large party hall. We all sat round a long round table. Some of the teachers made speeches and expressed happiness for my coming. I also spoke, and when the principal pointed to a female English teacher to tell him what I said, she was instead angry and said she understood nothing. You know, many Chinese say foreigners speak too fast for them to understand what they say. After eating the food that was prepared, the party closed at 10 pm and everyone went to their rooms. There was no internet connection in the school, but they did their best to provide me with an internet connection during my first week of stay there. They also provided me with a desktop computer. And the school installed a cable for me to watch international TV stations. All these things were for me alone. I was the foreign teacher, so the other teachers understood not to compare and they stayed naturally quiet.

The school gave me an opportunity to eat free meals at the teachers' restaurant. This was good for me. Because I had free lodging and meals, my salary was destined to pay my debt at my medical school. However, teaching English as a foreign teacher was not an easy task. The students had learnt very little English and so could not understand much. And I could not speak Chinese. The school further complexified things by grouping the children in classes according to their level of intelligence. It was challenging in the classes with the less intelligent ones, or at least I was brought to believe that. Because we did not understand each other, I got bored in front of the class, and the students had little to contribute.

However, in the classrooms with the intelligent students, it was interesting because the children understood some English and some of them could really express themselves powerfully. I did not understand this kind of class partition. When students are placed somewhere as the less intelligent ones, I think this kills self-esteem and the desire to learn. The boys in those classes felt they had to grow up faster, quit school and became taxi drivers; meanwhile the girls felt they had to grow up, quit school and serve food and drinks in restaurants. Then it became an ego problem in the intelligent group classrooms. When others were reading, you could sleep because "I am intelligent, I am intelligent," until the last day, when you realize you failed. Intelligence has to be matched with hard work. Therefore, I am of the opinion that mixing up the so called intelligent and the less intelligent students in the same classroom is better than separating them.

The school principal and the school in general expected wonders from a foreign English teacher. The school principal thought the foreign teacher was a magician whose presence would make the students start singing English. He thought that with my presence in his school, the students would become English specialists and his school would be a role model for other schools. When he watched TV and saw students in Beijing and other cities speak English like weaverbirds, he failed to understand that that was the result of many years of hard work since childhood. He did not understand why with the presence of a foreign English teacher in his school, with the presence of "Tardif from Holland" in his school, his students could not improve their level of English in one month. This was bad news for the principal. Some of his staff never agreed on hiring a foreign teacher. Some of the school staff was against this idea, but the principal was strongly for his dream of a foreign teacher to become a reality. This camp against the principal said it was a waste of money and resources hiring a foreign teacher. That it would be expensive to pay and host him in the school.

The principal eventually felt the foreign teacher had betrayed him. After my stay in the school for just one month, the camp against the principal at last had something to say. The school was paying the teacher a high salary, and they had not seen the change the principal promised. The principal stood defenceless. Nevertheless, although things never went as swiftly as the principal would have expected, he congratulated me many times for doing my work wholeheartedly. I took my work seriously. I was always on time and never missed any of my classes. I failed only where human limitations could not succeed. The principal called on all other teachers in the school to copy my example of a hard working person.

One day the medical school in Taiyuan sent James to come and see how everything was with me there in Xiang Yuan. This was because the visa I was carrying in my passport was that of the medical school showing that I was a student of the school. Because I was carrying a visa of the medical school, if anything happened to me elsewhere, the school was responsible. Therefore, they had to follow me up to be sure everything was fine. In addition, if the police caught me teaching in a school far away in another city while carrying a passport showing I was a medical student in their school, they had to pay heavy fines. They felt uneasy letting me go to do this job. When James came, he saw that everyone was happy with me. All the teachers and students were happy. There was peace, so he returned to Taiyuan very satisfied.

Then because the other foreigner never came with me, the school was silently shopping for another one to replace him. At the beginning of the second month, another black man joined me, and we had to work together in the school for the rest of the three months. His name was Ken. At this time media people came and interviewed us and left. Little did I know that that was the beginning of trouble. When police saw the interview broadcast on TV, they sent news to the school principal that he should bring the foreign teachers to the police station. When the school principal heard this news, he panicked and informed my medical school what the police demanded. The medical school reacted immediately by calling me to abandon the job and come at once to Taiyuan.

If the police landed in number 1 middle school, they would find faults with so many things, and the school and the foreign teachers would have to pay heavy fines. With lions' teeth, the police could find fault and tear number 1 middle school, the foreign teachers and the medical school into pieces. Number 1 middle school did not have the right authorizations to hire foreign teachers. I had but a student visa, which did not allow me to work. And the school I was attending was many hundreds of kilometres away. Therefore, the medical school as well would be in problems. The newly recruited foreign teacher, Ken, was carrying an "F" visa, which was a business visa. Everything was odd. And out of order before the law.

Number 1 middle school's principal was passionate about taking on foreign teachers. But he never made the effort to find out what it took hire such teachers. And all this eventually put trouble at the door. Schools that did not have the proper authorizations had to hire foreign teachers on a part time basis, not as full time teachers. When number 1 middle school met me, they were so excited and drafted a very nice contract with well-defined terms. When I thought about this later, it was funny to me because they just heard that a person came from Holland, drafted a contract, and signed him in without even seeing any identification.

With all the confusion going on, I was already in Taiyuan under the invitation of the medical school. Mr. Wang Wen Xue followed me to Taiyuan as a representative of number 1 middle school for negotiation of my visa situation. God made some souls support each other when facing trials and difficulties in life. Mr. Wang was an angel guiding and giving me full support in this depressed period of my life. I hold him in memory every day, and I hope to meet him in China one day and speak just two words to him, "Thank you." If I never meet him to say these words, I shall be disgruntled until my last day.

Well, despite the coming of Mr. Wang, the medical school told me they did not want to confront the police. They said they would not let me to keep staying with my passport carrying the visa of the medical school because if anything were to happen, it would cost them too much. Therefore, on November 3, 2005, the medical school took me to the police station and got my visa cancelled. I was given me an "L" visa – that was a tourist visa and had nothing to do with the medical school. The medical college was free from the nightmare. I had given them a lot of trouble, and they felt released from the invisible strings that tied them and me together. I had to go my way. My tourist visa was valid only for two weeks. I had to fight on to see if I could change it to an extended "F" visa. Usually "L" lasted only for very short periods, usually for weeks, but an "F" visa could last for even one year.

While I was in Taiyuan crying the death of my visa, Ken called me and told me the police finally came to number 1 middle school in my absence. The police asked for his passport, and he brought it forward. There it was carrying an "F" visa, therefore not authorized to work, and everyone saw he was Cameroonian and not Canadian as everyone in the school knew. The principal was very angry we had lied to him. This was a new scandal. The police asked for me, and they said I was in Taiyuan.

I returned to number 1 middle school with the "L" visa. The school authorities asked this time for my passport and knew I came from Cameroon and not Holland. The principal of the school was so angry. He sent a teacher to come and tell us we should leave the school. I asked, "How about the contract we signed?" I told the principal that if he failed to respect the contract, it would not be good for him because I

51

would win him at court. The principal was confused and did not know what to say. I also told the principal that the medical school cancelled my visa because of him, and now I had no visa, and he was telling me to leave. Leave to where? Although I said all that, at the back of my mind I was afraid. I was a frustrated man. The truth was that I could do nothing to the principal because I was not carrying the right visa for work. People work in China with a "Z" visa; as I was not carrying the work visa there was nothing I could do to the principal. However, what could a dying man like me do? I was frustrated and frightened. I found myself stranded in a foreign land.

If you are tired of swimming and find a stick in the middle of the ocean, what would you do? You would certainly hang onto the stick. I was tired in the middle of the ocean, and number 1 middle school was the stick I spotted, and the principal of number 1 middle school was the biggest and strongest branch. I spotted this opportunity, and I would not let myself drown. I fought like a wounded lion. When the police heard I had returned from Taiyuan, they came to see me too. They met me and asked a few questions like, "Why did you come to China?" and "When your contract is over here where will you go?" Then I am sure they fixed out everything with the school authorities, got their own money and left.

Meanwhile I called Mr. Thomson in Taiyuan to brief him about my situation. To tell him what I was going through. It was urgent to get my visa extended, yet I had no money. I thought, in such a situation, I needed to talk with someone, so we might find a solution. Mr. Thomson was the right person for me to talk to. He had accepted that I come and meet him in China some eight months ago. This was his reply in a text message, "I need to hear words of encouragement and thank you instead of words of despair." For me I was shocked to see this reply. A person I trusted was putting pepper in my wounds instead of iodine. I was thirsty and instead of giving me water, he gave me acid. I wondered what I did to deserve all that.

From the day I entered China, Mr. Thomson had failed me almost every other time I had counted on him. With whom could I talk, if I could not talk with a person who worked that I might come and meet him in China? This was bad luck. As if a heavy downpour was raining on me in the dry season. My situation was catastrophic. I expected Mr. Thomson to handle things differently. I was on fire. I was being burned. I suffered alone. I was in a faraway country, my family was far off, and there was nobody to talk to about my problems. Mr. Thomson, the closest person to me, had become a bulldog. He barked at whatever I said. I meditated and in a few days, I was surprised how my energies returned, and I was happy again. Depression was gone.

I sent my passport to Beijing to change it from an "L" visa to an "F" visa. Number 1 middle school had sent my salary straight to the medical school to reduce my debt. I did not even see it with my eyes, so I did not have money to pay as I sent my passport to Beijing. A woman I had known before leaving Taiyuan borrowed money for me, and I sent it to Beijing. But I had no way to pay back this money. The woman arranged a private class at her home, where I was teaching some children including her own son, until my debt was paid.

My passport finally arrived with an "F" visa in it. It was issued on November 24 and was valid until February 17 2006. Three months was not far off. Soon I would have to be renewing my visa again. From this period onwards, work at number 1 middle school went on well, until February when Ken and I had to leave, because our visas were going to expire. I did my work well hoping that somehow I would find a lasting solution for my problems. The teachers and students of the school were happy with me. Because only the foreign teachers had computers, in the evenings, the other teachers would come to my room and surf the internet, chat with QQ (a Chinese social network site) and play games. Although the students were not fast at learning English, they were nevertheless happy with foreign teachers around them.

Then the day came for our departure. We had grown fond of each other. The teachers and students did not want the departure day to come. Many of the students wept and some of the teachers also. We had become a family. It was difficult to part. I was almost playing the role of a pastor or priest in that school. Students would come up with all kinds of problems, even secret family matters, and ask for advice. I did the best I could. They never thought I would one day leave. When the students heard the principal saying we were Cameroonians, they rejected that idea with, "We love our teachers. Let them have peace."

7

Back to Taiyuan and the shock of seeing my visa expired

It was over at number 1 middle school. I returned to Taiyuan. I was confused. The medical school had taken most of what I had earned teaching for what I owed them. I paid 2500 Yuan ($350) to Mr. Thomson for what he lent to me for payment to the medical school. I had no money and no job, but I had to live. A woman I had known secured an apartment for me. She and her husband met me at the bus station and took me to that apartment. When we arrived there, I observed the neighbourhood, and it was terrible. All around were ancient dirty houses. I thought that if I had to live abroad outside my own country, it was not under these conditions. The Chinese observe foreigners. They respect foreigners very much, because a bulk of the population is unable to move out of China. They believe foreigners are well to do. So if I had to live in that kind of neighbourhood, probably everyone in the city would learn about me, a foreigner living in the dirtiest neighbourhood. This could not work. More so, I had just about a month for my "F" visa to run out. If everyone knew about me, it meant the police would come sniffing around.

In any case, we carried my luggage to my apartment on the third floor. It was a two-room apartment with a toilette and a kitchen. The apartment was not less filthy than the entire house and the neighbourhood. It was as if people had not lived there for decades. The apartment smelled like old stuff. It smelled like a haunted house. My heart was beating hard. I asked myself how I could live there. The funny thing was that, from that very spot where I was standing, I had no other place to go. This woman brought iron brushes, and we brushed the floors and walls and washed them with water and soap, but that smell never went away. For her, there was no problem with that apartment. I complained that I did not have money. She said if I did not have money, that apartment was the right choice, whether I was a foreigner or not. Even if I was from another planet, without money it was the right place for me. After living in the apartment for about a week or two, I abandoned it for another one. The new one was a single room apartment with a toilette and kitchen. It was small, but I did not care. At least it was a bit cleaner and had no strong old smells. Plus the neighbourhood was much better.

While in Taiyuan, in my new apartment, in the middle of winter, I took a shower one day with cold water. It was terrible. I felt as if my blood was not circulating. I felt almost frozen. I turned on the heater and heated myself. After about ten minutes, I felt ok. That experience taught me never to try a cold-water shower in winter again.

The day for my visa to expire was drawing near. That was to be on February 17, 2006, and it was already early February. What would I do? What could I do to get it extended for one year? That was the mystery question. I could not hope to have a work visa, because I could get a work visa only if I had a job in a school with an authorization to hire foreign teachers. Therefore, the hope was only for a business or "F" visa. There was a condition for renewing an "F" visa. If a foreigner lives in China for one year, he or she must leave China, return with another entry visa, and extend it again. That was the rule. Therefore, I had to leave mainland China and travel to a neighbouring country to obtain another entry visa. I had entered China in March 2005, and it was already February 2006. Immigration law was catching up with me. I had to go to neighbouring Mongolia or Macao and get another entry visa at the Chinese embassy and then re-enter China and extend my visa for another year or so.

I had very little money with me, so I could not afford to travel to any of China's neighbours. Though I was frustrated, I still entertained hopes about finding an opportunity to get the problem resolved. Mr. Thomson told me there was a possibility to get my visa done in Guangzhou, in China's Guangdong Province. He had been in China longer than I, and he had more experience solving these kinds of problems. I gave him my passport on February 13 with 2000 Yuan ($250), and he told me he would send it to Guangzhou to get it done. There were only three days left before the expiration of my visa. He gave me all the assurances about getting my visa renewed. Because he had given me all those assurances, I did not get in touch with him for the three remaining days. Suddenly on February 18, I received a call from Mr. Thomson who said, "Your visa donc born." That is Pidgin English meaning, "Your visa has expired."

I met him, and he gave me new assurances that it was still possible to get the visa done, that there was no problem. He then sent the passport, maybe to Guangzhou again, to be renewed. One day in early March 2006, Mr. Thomson called me to come and get my passport with my new visa. I was busy on that day, so I didn't go. The next day, he called and spoke as if on fire: "Come get your passport from me. What is your passport doing in my hands?" By these words, I understood. He realized things were bad, so he wanted the passport out of his hands as soon as possible. He wanted to wash his conscience clear of my problems. He did not want to find himself one day accountable for my failed resident status in China. I rode my bicycle to his apartment. I got my passport, opened it and saw the visa page. There was the new visa, an "L" visa, issued on March 1, 2006 and valid until March 31, 2006. It was another tourist visa, valid only for one month. What a joke.

I rode my bike back to my apartment. I was not used to riding the bike in winter like the Chinese. When I did, I always caught cold. I could not compare with the Chinese. I had to suffer the consequences. It was not my entire body, but just my hands and fingers. Despite the gloves I wore while riding, they were icy – almost frozen. Any microorganisms living on them I am sure abandoned them to look for a new source of life. I could not feel my hands and fingers, yet they were extremely painful. I opened my heater and heated them. Within a few minutes, I felt life slowly returning to the ends of my arms. I felt the blood circulating again. My fingertips rejoiced.

At this point, I realized I had to face the reality of China. I had to face reality on the ground. At the ninetieth minute, a crazy team should still be hoping to score three goals to defeat a powerful opponent. What could I do at this point in my game? A one-month "L" visa was nothing. One month would come in the blink of an eye. I had no money. I had gone through stress, and the result was a one-month tourist visa. It was no use. It would have been better to save the $250. The way Mr. Thomson pushed my passport to me on that day, I realized there were no hopes. I observed how his hands panicked. I wondered why. Maybe something told him that the man who follows you to China does not receive the best of you. I was guessing. I said nothing.

I sat in my room later that day with questions. Should we trust peoples' words when they speak? Is it part of human nature to speak words and never follow them? Should I doubt promises and other things people say? Should I become a doubting Thomas? No doubt the name of my father was Thomas. I could not provide answers to these questions. Maybe Fonlon or Socrates could. I knew the one-month renewal of my visa would lead quickly to a situation of expiration and renewed frustration. I had no money to go to Mongolia or Macao to get an entry visa. I prepared my mind. The end of March came, and the visa was expired, as I expected.

I was without a visa. I could not find work. To find even a part time job was a problem. Most blacks who had not developed roots in China faced the same situation. Not the white man however. I had a few tutorial classes that helped me pay my rents and buy food. One day, a friend, a black lady, told me there was a Chinese English teacher who wanted to learn and improve his English. She gave me his number and I called him. One morning we arranged for a place and met. We met and agreed to go to my apartment and have the first class. He bought some apples for me. He carried the apples in a plastic bag. On the way to my house, the plastic burst from the bottom and the apples poured to the ground. We gathered the apples, but my intuition told me that was a bad sign for the classes. I felt something would go wrong.

We reached my apartment, and I realized my student had very, very bad body odour. I opened all the windows for fresh air to come in. Yet it was still not easy. I was still trying to cope with the smell when I observed something funny. Everywhere I sat in my room, this man jumped like a frog and met me there. I wondered if we were at an English lesson or a frog dance lesson. I did not understand what it was all for. My first intention for not wanting to sit near him was because of his strong body smell. Otherwise, what was wrong with another human sitting by another? I thought he was unaware of his body odour and wanted us to sit close before studying English. Each time I changed my position, I was also trying to ask him what he wanted to learn in English, whether it was general or specifics. My questions were nothing to him. Everything was about his frog dance. Then maybe he realized I did not understand what he wanted, so he added one more move to the dance. Each time he jumped and met me where I was, he tapped with his palms the front of my trousers, where my manhood hung. With the new style, I understood what he came for. This thing was not English learning. I remembered the apple tragedy.

Despite the fact that I understood, it was still difficult for me to cope with such a character. I had heard of gay people, but I never knew one personally. However, I was determined to stay cool. I told him I understood him now but that we should have the English lesson. He replied, "No, English is not important. I lover you." I stayed cool, and I wanted to know something about him. I told him we should talk first, that there was no problem. I asked him what made him gay. He said when he was in middle school he lived in his dormitory room with another boy. He and his roommate became lovers. Then after middle school, he never met his lover again. He said he grew used to men, and he wanted to have only boyfriends.

I told him he should try a woman. He told me women have no place in the romantic part of his being. That they are like lifeless stones and wood to him. He apparently had no

60

feelings at all for women. When I saw his story was finished, I told him, "This is our first meeting, so we cannot do anything today. Let's wait for our next meeting." When I spoke those words, it was as if I had poured petrol on fire. It was like uttering the name of Jesus in hell. He grinded his teeth and twisted his eyes. I saw that his eyes became fixed. I told myself that the English lesson would pull off my head! He stood fixed, looked paralyzed, and was gazing at me straight in the eyes. I thought, if he collapsed in my apartment what would I do. I also thought, in that state of almost paralysis, if he launched a heavy blow at me what would I do, and if I became unconscious with that blow, what would happen.

With these thoughts in mind, I quickly grabbed my keys and picked up my backpack. I jumped straight to the door and told him I had a class to teach and must go. He grinded his teeth again and said with a weeping voice, "No, you cannot do that." I insisted until he finally realized I was very serious. I was neither missing, nor mixing my words. I observed how his eyes relaxed, and the black spot moved and no longer fixed as before. I noticed how he got relaxed, and I could read signs of defeat in his entire personality. However, I could not relax my voice because I was still afraid, so I kept shouting until he walked out.

I locked my door, went to the street, called the lady and informed her that the English lesson was not about English but a hungry man burning with desire. Though he left, he continued to send messages to me that he loved me. He stopped when I told him I would tell the lady who sent him to me. Well, in any case, I had nothing against this man or his sexual orientation. It is not for me to decide whether a person is homosexual or heterosexual. The thing was that he approached me with what I had never been oriented for and I could not change. I was not asking his opinion. It was my right and I stood on what I wanted. I never felt good about that experience. I went to China to study Chinese medicine and return to Africa and help my people. But I got frustrated and was not seeing my way, especially when men of desire started coming.

Time wore on. I picked up a few part time jobs, and I had no problem paying for my one-room apartment, my food, and my water and electricity bills. I had an excellent friend, Dr. Song Younqing, who arranged private classes for me and helped me with almost everything I needed to do in town. I visited him and his wife and son weekly. I also visited his parents and got to know his entire family. When I knew his entire family, I was surprised to realize something new. The family circle of the Chinese is so small, a heavy contrast to African families. All family members of my friend amounted to just eleven. I could actually count them. This was so shocking to me, because the entire family of each African family can be in the hundreds. Yes, not just one hundred, but many hundreds. Contrary to the Chinese, the African husband and his wives are multiplication machines for "God said go and multiply."

My girlfriend Na, whom I fell in love with a few months after entering China, was of great help to me too. With the language barrier, I could not do everything I wanted to do. She would go around with me, and we would do things together. We would go around by bus or by bike, and the days moved on.

It was already two months since my visa expired. I thought, if the police were to catch me and repatriate me, what would become of me. What would I take home with me? What had I gained from China? Having enough to eat everyday was not enough, I thought. I started searching online to find a distance learning college. I searched for schools offering distance learning in Chinese medicine and found one in Beijing. This school was MEDBOO (Beijing institute of traditional Chinese medicine). They were offering the study of Chinese medicine online, and the fees were moderate. I could pay for them with what I earned from my tutorial classes. I thought this was the best thing I could do. If anything bad was to happen and I returned to Cameroon, then I could heal the sick from what I would learn. For this reason, by June 2006, I paid the fees through a Chinese friend as I could not use my passport. I began the studies, but I did not have a computer. I had to go to the net bar and download the notes, print them in book form and read at home. Writing the exams was tedious, because I had to stay in the net bar and write there.

In any case, I did not give up. I learnt all the courses and eventually was to successfully complete them in May 2008. With all what I learnt by that time, I was qualified to treat patients with the various traditional therapeutic methods. At least I was to be satisfied in this direction.

Meanwhile, the days passed, and my adventure was on-going. In my sleep, something would whisper in my ears, in a very low tone, "Tardif, walk this adventure to the end, never fear."

8

The period of September 2006 to July 2007

I had kept up with my few tutorial classes until September 2006 when luck stroke. That September, I picked up part time teaching jobs at the Taiyuan normal college, Taiyuan University and a middle school. All that in addition to my many private classes. This was already a lot of work. I could actually make and save some money this time. I was able to change my one-room apartment to a two-room apartment. As far as my love life, my girlfriend was a very traditional Chinese girl. Although I visited her family several times, she never hoped to marry a foreigner. She liked to assist me in whatever I wanted to do, but the idea of marrying a foreigner was not very strong in her mind. Because I was seriously thinking of finding a girl I could marry, naturally things had to die down somehow between us. This does not mean we were enemies. We still visited each other, as before, and went around together, but that zeal of thinking about marriage was not there.

This naturally pushed me to fall in love with another girl called Zhao in November 2006. Zhao was completely different from me. She was so crazy. She could not do nor think of anything serious. Her mind was so unstable and inconsistent. She was not a serious student at school. Unfortunately, I was not that kind of a crazy person. We fell in love in November 2006 and by March 2007 the relationship was dying down almost completely. At first she withdrew from me. I relentlessly attempted to keep her by my side but to no avail. Then it reached a stage where I too started withdrawing. Then she attempted coming back to me, but I knew it was a waste of time, so I withdrew out of it completely. The final blow was in March 2007.

Before she met me, she had another boyfriend, a German man. She kept that relationship going. He was financially better off than I was. Before meeting me, she expected all foreigners to be the same; that is all foreigners are rich and enjoy the high life. Then she realized I was not rich like the German. The German left China in March 2007, and she expected me to fill the gap he had left in her life, by taking her on trips from one city to another, going to expensive hotels and eating in very expensive restaurants. The German had already taught her luxury and high life. I preached untiringly that life was not all like that, but she would not listen. My preaching was useless. She saw in me a kind of philosophy of life that could not hold her. And I could not change to her kind of lifestyle. Even if I had the money, I would not go crazy the way she wanted. I was stubborn to change to her lifestyle, and she stubborn to change to mine. We were two extremes. If we continued to meet, there would be explosions. Therefore, I surrendered the relationship and despite the fact that she made a few attempts to meet me, I knew it was not for the better, so things finally died down by April 2007.

Despite this break in my relationship with Zhao, I was still doing well for jobs. However, this was not without problems and resistance from the students I taught. It was somehow troublesome to teach English in China. We Africans pose as Americans and British to find work, but no matter how much you pretend, you shall never have the American or British accent of British and American natives. A clean accent, clear pronunciation and speaking tone are very important to be able to teach English successfully in China. I was not an exception. The Chinese students protest against you, everything about you. They do not want you to teach them, they do not like you. I faced this resistance in my workplaces just as many other teachers of English in China did and still do.

I stood my ground wherever I went for work, did my best. The students finally accepted me as their teacher. However, in one of the schools, the students protested to an extent that I could not stand it. Therefore, I told the woman who was in charge of the English department that I wanted to drop the job. I did not want to go back there again. If I had somewhere better to go, I would have left immediately, but I had nowhere to go. She and one of the excellent students in English encouraged me to return and continue, saying there would be no more problems. I did and surprisingly that school ended up being the best school that I taught in, in China. The students and I became best friends, and it was so wonderful to be with them. As time went by, my confidence grew, and I was able to pick up work anywhere and work without such resistance. However, the beginning in China is very frightening, and you just wished you had never gone there.

Though confidence had grown in me, and I had enough work and money too, my visa was still a problem. I had no visa. What would I do to have it done? I asked myself this question every day in China. It was already April 2007, and that made me already one year in China without a valid visa. One day I went to send some money back home to Cameroon. I begged for Mr. Thomson's passport to do so, and he was so kind to give me his passport to use. The young lady I met at the money transfer office opened the passport and noticed the photo was not mine. I observed her. As she looked at the passport, she also looked at me. Then while looking at me, I saw she picked up the phone to call someone. I immediately understood what she wanted to do – call the authorities, maybe the police or the immigration department.

I stopped her and called Mr. Thomson immediately. I told him how the lady suspected me and wanted to call the authorities. I told him to explain to the girl that he was busy and wanted me to make a transfer for him. Mr. Thomson's Chinese was so perfect. I handed the phone to the lady, and she spoke with Mr. Thomson. I saw she was satisfied. I learnt my lesson. From that day onwards, each time I had to send money out of China, I never did it personally but via a Chinese friend. This lady had a right to feel things were awry. People carry passports of others and use them as their own.

A certain Chinese once approached me to propose I buy a passport of a certain Ghanaian with a valid visa in it. If I bought it, I would have to bear the name in the passport and the Ghanaian nationality. I thought of this, but my conscience troubled me a lot. Maybe the person is dead somewhere or suffering somewhere, and I would be carrying his passport. I did not really feel like going that far just to be able to live in China. Moreover, the passport he proposed carried just a three-month visa. There was no point.

In March 2007, there was a possibility for me to travel to Inner Mongolia and get a new entry visa. This was supposed to cost about 1 000 000 FCFA ($2000). Getting another entry visa was only one step. To then extend the visa still needed other money, about 300 000 FCFA ($600). This was a risky deal, because I could get the visa extended perhaps for only three months instead of a year and be so unfortunate to see it expire again. Despite this, I was thinking seriously of travelling to Inner Mongolia to get this visa issue resolved.

At this point, I received a message from home in Cameroon that the interest on the money I borrowed at home when I was leaving in 2005 was already too much. My mother told me I needed to pay the money urgently. The amount I had to pay was about five times more than the amount I originally borrowed. It therefore meant that if I did not pay the money, it would keep increasing. I thought that if I used the money I had, travelled and got another entry visa but failed to extend it for a long time, then it would still expire and the debt in Cameroon would still be there. I finally decided to send the money back home and pay the debt. I cleared this debt and peace returned to me. There was a big risk for me to stay in China still owing this money. This was because in case I had a problem and was to be repatriated, what would I do while owing that money. It would not go well for me. In addition, my mother told me the person I borrowed the money from was constantly demanding his money. After two years and no news from me, naturally he was afraid that maybe I might never pay up. I never regretted the decision to pay this money instead of going for the visa.

Because I had accumulated several good part time jobs, by early May 2007 I had raised some money again. Though the money was not enough, I wanted to see where I could get some assistance and try getting the visa done. In this vein, I asked Mr. Thomson to lend me some money so I could pay him back when I received my salary at the end of May. He told me there was no problem and that he would lend me the money. I told him I was to travel on the weekend. He agreed with me very well, but on that Saturday, when I had prepared my little bag to travel to Beijing, I called him and told him I was ready to go. That I would pass by his house to get the money. What a surprise. He told me there was no money to give me. I was confused. Had I known I would have this kind of disappointment, I would have tried getting the money from some other friends. I was completely confused why this should have happened. Why did he not inform me this money would not be available? Why did he let me come to China when even under very stressful conditions he could not extend a helping hand to me?

Thousands of thoughts and questions came to my mind, but I never found answers to them. From this point in my life, I understood how certain things work. I never again attempted to have any kind of financial dealings with Mr. Thomson. The opportunity to leave China and get my visa done in Inner Mongolia or Macao was blocked. I was not lucky. China closed all its boarders, and I never had an opportunity to leave the country and get my visa done. Even when I later had the money, it was impossible to cross the border and return with a visa. What could I do? I was doomed to stay for good or for bad without that visa.

When Mr. Thomson disappointed me on that day, the sadness in me sank deeper. I suddenly felt that humans should not live up to old age before learning to be alone. Alone in the sense that man or woman should not hope to rely so much on others to resolve problems he or she is facing. This does not also mean we should stay without companions and family members around us. In many ways, man or woman is alone in the sense that we have to decide mostly by ourselves on how to go about resolving the problems we face. I came to understand why some older people I met lived the way they did; life had taught them how to be alone. They told me they hate to rely on others. They wanted to be able to do their things by themselves, until they were completely worn out or unable to do so anymore.

I once met a man who was over seventy-five years old. He was married in his youth and had many children. Those children turned against him. They tormented him and could give him nothing. They could not help him in any way. I visited him frequently. He worked in the farms alone, cooked his food by himself and tapped his palm wine by himself, which he drank. He told me that all humans must learn to survive by themselves. If you relied on others, even on your own children, they would fail you when you most expected help. He was an example. Fighting for survival at seventy-five is not an easy thing to think of.

Then I met another old man about that same age. I visited him frequently. He had his wives and children at home. I observed that each time he ate he washed the plate after eating. I also saw him many times take his clothes and wash them personally. I asked him why he was washing the dishes and his clothes by himself, at that age, when he had children at home. He told me that everyone must learn to be alone. Learn to do your things by yourself if you still have the energy. He told me that if you learn to do things by yourself, it makes you strong and you will be able to face life when you are abandoned. However at one point, you might be tired due to disease or age. God would know you have the zeal to do but lack the strength.

On the day in China of my deception with Mr. Thomson, I saw these two people before me as if in visions. Their words were pounding in my mind as if they were some powerful teachings from Mount Sinai. I became more flexible in the way I saw people. I did not trust peoples' words so much when they promised to carry on any business with me the way I used to trust before. With this understanding, when people fail in their promises to me, I take it easy rather seeing it as a do or die affair.

The disease I suffered from I ended up calling the "African Hereditary Disease" (AHD). This disease runs in the blood and veins of more than 90% of all African people. This disease is the disease of "expectancy from relatives and friends." I suffered heavily from this disease. We in Africa make our plans relying on relatives, friends, friends of relatives and so on. We hope and rely heavily on family and family friends and believe strongly they will resolve our problems. We hope they will raise us to where we hope to be. Some of the causes of this disease are poverty and large family sizes. Because family sizes are large, parents find it difficult to take care of all their children. It is difficult for them to pay all the school fees and hospital bills and feed and clothe their children. For these reasons, when the children are young, parents expect relatives and friends to come and take care of the needs of the very children they have birthed.

The children see what happens from childhood, so when they are growing up they already know they have to seek for help elsewhere. From the age of puberty, the children are actively engaged in seeking help from all quarters of the globe. Parents and children expect other relatives and friends to pay their fees at school, pay their hospital bills and help them learn a trade. There is no limit to what poorer parents and children expect from relatives. The relatives who are successful are not many in every family. They are few while the entire family is large. So naturally it is difficult for those few to take care of everyone in the family. And these few successful people are already married and raising their own children. They have to take care of their immediate family. It is therefore difficult for those gainfully employed to take care of the rest of the populous family. Yet in situations where they fail to satisfy the relatives, these relatives curse them as wicked, selfish and destined for hell, for their money is shit.

I suffered heavily from this disease. Not that I cursed anyone, but when I graduated from high school and my mother could not pay my fees at university, I expected a certain relative or family friend from somewhere to come and say, "Come and let me sponsor you at university." Despite the fact that I had already stayed at home for seven years, the thought that I would soon be going to university by some relative's help never left me. Most Africans suffer from this disease. When they fail to get what they want, after some years, they give up and start cursing the rich relatives day and night. In my case however, I never gave up but kept hoping no matter how long it would have taken me. This thought that a certain relative was coming to solve my problem hung heavily on me at all times. When in the farms, on the road, and in my bed, I could not kill this thought.

This disease left me one day in an instant. The cure came to me as a bomb. It fell heavily on me, and I saw where I had gone wrong over the years. Waiting and hoping to catch the wind. Yes, catch the wind. This disease left me the day Mr. Thomson failed his promise to me. On that day I felt this disease flying out of me like a butterfly. I felt some freedom. I felt that I had always attached myself to what was not real. This disease left me, and until all the days of my life, I am sure it will not return. Most Africans lack the cure for this disease and eventually die with this hereditary disease of expectancy, even unfortunately in their old age.

9

Black Thursday, 25 July 2007

In the summer of 2007, I was free, as all the students had gone home on holidays. I was busy studying my online courses in traditional Chinese medicine. A man and his fiancée approached me and suggested I go and teach a one-month summer camp class. They had organized this class in Gao Ping, a small city in Shanxi Province. I was afraid to leave Taiyuan city. To live without a visa in the city is far safer than to live in a village. In the city, there are many foreigners. Unless there is a kind of scandal, nobody pays much attention on you. However, in a small place, where maybe you are even the first foreigner to set foot there, news gets around about you like wildfire. The police could come and problems would begin.

With my new girlfriend, Rong, I met the couple. Because I needed to keep working to keep making money, I decided to take the risk and went in for the job. It was around July 7, 2007 that I set off for Gao Ping. The class was supposed to last for one month. We arrived in Gao Ping. The house I had to live in was terrible. The toilette was a pit latrine and it was so bad. I had no choice. I needed money and I would have to work to have money. This couple said they would pay me at the end of the class. We began the classes. The children were very young – between the ages of six and ten. It was the first time they were meeting a foreigner. The children were very excited, and the classes were going well. The couple that hired me was happy.

One afternoon on my return from class, there was a truck at the home I was living in. The air was so stinky. I asked what was wrong, and they told me the truck, with a pipe extended into the latrine, was draining the shit from it. I had to get away but did not know where to go. I went searching until I ended up in a net bar. I spent the rest of the day there. On my return at night, the air was still stenchy and unbearable. I never felt good in that home. The air was never normal again.

However, my class was going on well until one Thursday morning. Every morning I would chose my tarot card of the day. My card of the day that morning was the king of cups. I felt good when I chose that card. So I was king on that day, a king and a loving father, I thought. It would be a good day, a very good day indeed. Unfortunately, that day would not be governed by the great king and loving father as I thought. It was the opposite. We had already had the class for two weeks, and two weeks were remaining. I prayed to my god that the next two weeks would be as tranquil.

On that Thursday, 25 July 2007, I was teaching my class. Suddenly at 9 am, I was told by the lady who hired me to stop. That some people wanted to see me in the office. I met them there, and they told me they were the police and wanted my passport. They also questioned why I was in their district. I told them I did not carry my passport with me because I feared losing it. I also explained that I was in their district because it was the holiday, and my boss invited me to follow her and help the children learn English. They immediately charged me for teaching illegally in their district and living in their district without a passport. They also told my boss that the class as an illegal class. Thus, the class was officially over, and I was under arrest.

To the police at Gao Ping, a foreigner in their detention was a high profile case, so they had to call the main police station at Jin Cheng, maybe one hundred or fewer kilometres from Gao Ping. When they called Jin Cheng, the police head said they should come with me to Jin Cheng. They took me to my room to get ready. While in my room, I did some meditation and asked divine providence to free me out of the hands of the police so I could return to Taiyuan city. When I finished my meditations, I came out and met the men who stood all around where I was living. I discreetly called Mr. Thomson, and he told me to escape. I told him they were all around me, and I could not escape.

Three police carried my boss and me in their car to Jin Cheng. It was about a forty-five minute drive. We arrived at around 10:30 am. They took me to the office and kept my boss out. The first thing they did was take photos of me. Then they began questioning me. They asked my name and my country. I told them my name and told them I came from Cameroon. When the police officers who brought me from Gao Ping heard me say I was a Cameroonian, they laughed and said in Gao Ping they were told I was American. They were happy that the truth would come out now. They repeated the question why I was in Gao Ping. I told them what I said before, that it was the holiday and I was invited to come and help the children learn English. They asked for my passport, and I told them my passport was in Taiyuan. They asked what I was doing in Taiyuan. I told them I was teaching, and learning Chinese medicine. They asked for my names and passport number. I think I gave them my true names, but I never gave them my true passport number.

They searched their computers repeatedly for my names and passport and found nothing about me. They kept searching for hours but found nothing. They called my boss into the office and questioned her too. Then they returned into their computers to search for information about me. Each time they found nothing. After hours of searching, they would ask again for my passport number. Most of the time I had forgotten the previous number I gave, so each time I would give but a different number off the top of my head. They would begin the search and still find nothing. The policewoman doing the search was a young officer. I thought she would discover I was giving different passport numbers each time. But each time she took the number, she said nothing. I thought it would be hell on me if they discovered I was giving different numbers. I did not really know what was happening. Might the woman understand yet want to be sympathetic? I did not know.

I lay on a bench in their office, as I was stressed up and tired. All along, however, I was extremely calm. I feared nothing and did not panic. Already in the hands of the police, I knew there was very little chance for me to walk out of the situation. Despite this, I did not give up with silent meditations, and with autosuggestions like, "I will return to Taiyuan city today safe and sound." I did all the meditations I knew and knew that all things were still possible. I was in touch with Mr. Thomson. I had run out of air time credit, so he was calling me every twenty minutes to get updates about my situation. I had some money that I had kept in my apartment. And I instructed him what to do with the money, like using part to pay my fines for an illegal stay and also to buy my flight ticket back home.

The police kept searching until 5 o'clock in the evening and found nothing. Then they asked me to give them the name of the school where I was teaching in Taiyuan. I gave them the name of one of them: Taiyuan Normal College. They asked me for a contact number at the school. I gave them the number of the English teacher who headed the English department, Mrs. Hu. The head of police at the Jin Cheng police station called her and asked her to fax my passport pages to him. I sat and observed how he was very serious, but I knew that nothing better would come from the normal college. This was because I gave to the normal college only my school certificates, and the first page of my passport.

The police were very excited when they received a fax from Taiyuan at 6 o'clock, from Mrs. Hu. The police head brought the faxed documents to the police officer who understood English to tell him what they carried. After listening to the officer, I saw how angry the police head got. This was because the woman officer told him that they were my certificates. He said he asked for my passport and visa pages but the Taiyuan normal school sent him my certificates, and what use did he have for those. He got angry; I saw how he almost turned red. He must have thought that since he began work as a police officer, I was a high profile case and he was determined not to fail. It was already late. School offices would not stay open after 6 pm, so he could not keep asking the normal school to fax more documents.

When the police contacted Mrs. Hu, she told some of the teachers and students that I had run into trouble in Jin Cheng. Some teachers and students started calling and asking me what had happened. I said nothing much, that it was just a small misunderstanding and that all would be ok. I thought of my chosen tarot card for that day, King of cups. I saw no danger for that day. I hoped things would still be ok.

The police searched the internet relentlessly. It was already dark. They were searching and compiling the report of my case at the same time. I lay, tired and tried, on the bench in their office. I had had a little tea that morning, but that is all I had had all day. I meditated, and thought of my new girlfriend Rong. We had fallen in love just a week ago. Thousands of things ran across my mind. Falling in love with a young man and then him getting caught by the police and being repatriated would be a shocking experience for her. I thought of this regretfully. It would have been better we had never fallen in love, I thought. Then I reflected on how I would soon be back in Cameroon. I would be unemployed, poor and bankrupt, but I had paid all my debts. I did not owe anybody and that was ok.

The police remained glued to the computer searching, and I stayed on that bench, now and then stepping out to answer calls. I stayed with them in that office until 11 pm when they found nothing. They themselves got tired too. They opted to give up for the night and continue the next day. They took us to a restaurant that night where all of us had a meal together. We ate and chatted there happily as if we were friends, as if there was nothing at loggerheads. My boss and I offered to pay for the meal, which offer the police head rejected. He paid. After the meal, the police head instructed the police officers who took us to Jin Cheng to return with us to Gao Ping, spend the night there and return the next morning to Jin Cheng.

We arrived in Gao Ping at 12:30 am. My boss and I thought the police would take me to their station to pass the night there. To our surprise, they came and left us at the home where we were staying and said we should report to their station at 7 am so that we go back to Jin Cheng. My boss had already informed her husband about what had happened. When we arrived in Gao Ping, he had arrived and had already bought my train ticket. There was a train due to pass through Gao Ping at 2 am en route to Taiyuan city. The train would stop at Gao Ping, take on passengers and continue. At 1:20 am, we went to the train station and waited for the train. The train finally arrived at 2 am as expected, and I got in. I had no seat. I stood up until we arrived in Taiyuan at 8 am. From the train station, I took a taxi to my apartment. I was so tired. I took a shower and went to bed. I woke up at 2 pm and went back to the city for a walk.

My boss later met me in Taiyuan. She told me they reported my escape to the police. The police were so angry and asked them to pay a heavy fined which they did. I lost all the financial benefits that were to fall from the class I was teaching. From that period onwards, fear and only fear occupied my mind. Would they come to Taiyuan to follow me up there? That was the next question.

10

September 2007 to June 15, 2008, the day I left China

I was afraid to keep staying in Taiyuan city. I thought about leaving Shanxi Province for another province of China, but many things came to mind. I had roots in Taiyuan already. I had friends. I knew people who could help me in my daily activities. I had jobs in Taiyuan that I found it hard to abandon. It was very hard to find work in China. If I went to another city, I would have to find work afresh, new friends and so on. How was I to find work in a new city? To start from ground level in China is a hell of a problem. It was very difficult to predict what might happen. How was the security situation in other cities? I had no idea. If I didn't leave Taiyuan, couldn't I live there quietly without a major incident?

In the end, despite all the fear, I decided to stay in Taiyuan city. I thought I should not panic and go to live in places I did not know. My life had become better financially, and I did not want fear about how to make money to take over my life again. I still had all my jobs in Taiyuan, why should I leave? I decided that police or no police, I would stay in Taiyuan. It was already September 2007 and schools reopened. I gave the name of the Taiyuan normal school to the police at Gao Ping and Jin Cheng. They knew I was teaching there. Would the police be coming to the school to find me? I thought that maybe I should abandon work there and continue work with the other schools. However, I was stubborn again. I thought how very difficult it was to find work and decided I was not going to abandon that job.

Therefore, in September 2007, I gathered up my courage and went to work in all the schools where I had obtained jobs. In the meantime, all the money I had with me was 600 000 FCFA ($1200). I sent this money back to Cameroon. The reason I did so was so that, in case the police arrested me and sent me home, when I arrived I would not be completely broke. In short, I would have a bit of money to live on for a few months. By that time, I had succeeded in buying a Toshiba laptop computer. With my laptop, I was able to study my traditional Chinese medicine online without difficulties. This saved me from going to net bars. I also paid all my fees for the course to guarantee that in case the police repatriated me, I could complete my studies while in Cameroon without major problems.

By this time, my students had a lot of confidence in me. It was less than two and a half years since I entered China. I had matured and was more experienced in handling the students and their problems. I had no fear whatsoever about losing any of my jobs. By the end of October 2007, I was teaching in four major schools in Taiyuan city. They were the Taiyuan normal college, Taiyuan University, You Shi College and a private middle school. It was the second year those schools confirmed me in the jobs, except for You Shi College which was a new job for me. Although it was a new job, I got it without difficulties because of my experience. In Taiyuan normal school, the students and I became very good friends. They were the very students that tried to reject me a year before. They loved me and could not accept a new teacher in my place. I felt good with them, and I felt as if it was best I spend all my life in China. I got so busy and could study medicine for only an hour or two every day. Aside of these schools where I taught, I also had many private classes.

All the students knew I was American. Three of the four schools where I taught were university level schools, and almost all the topics related to European and American culture, politics, and ways of life. We covered famous places in the United States of America and in the United Kingdom, differences between American and British cultures, and so on. It was general knowledge I was teaching. The students were so curious. They wanted to know things, everything around the world. I, standing before them, was an American. I had to tell them what they wanted to know. This was very challenging, but there was no problem, for I knew the tricks. After every class, we chose the topic for the next class the next day or next week. If the topic was let's say "famous places in, or sightseeing, in America," when I returned home, quiet in my room, I would browse the internet and get all sorts of things about the topic. Once I made a few notes, that was enough for me to go through the class without any problem. In my classes, I hardly ever ran into embarrassments.

In the beginning, I did not know how to turn around what I did not know. In one of my classes, the students one day suggested we talk about "Prison Break," an American TV series. I had never heard about it, so I asked, "What's prison break?" The students laughed. But because they loved me already, they overlooked my ignorance and did not hold it against me. If I had known the trick on how to go around these kinds of questions, I would have just stayed quiet and quickly switched the topic to another one. With time, it was so easy for me to shift from one idea, that I had no strong knowledge of, to another, without the students much noticing or at least commenting. Nevertheless, when I shifted like this, I always researched those unexpected and unknown topics later. And one day in class, I would come back to them. At least this helped the students learn what they actually loved to know.

Another trick I used, beginning at least in 2005 in the net bars in China, was to visit internet groups on American accent training. I realized later, because I used my real name, that savvy students on the internet could have seen some of my postings and asked me why, as an American, I was concerned with accent training. They never asked, but had they, I suppose I would have at first felt caught off guard but then been quick on my feet. I would have explained that my accent was innate and that I was looking for tips for them on how they might work to acquire that American accent they so sought.

Work went on well, but fear could not completely leave me. One morning as I got ready to go to work, I chose my tarot card for that day. This card would be a guide to my daily activities for the day. That morning, the card I chose was the ten of swords. Ten of swords meant problems for me on that day. I told myself that only a fool would chose this type of card and go out. I decided I would not leave my room all day. Calls came from the Taiyuan normal college saying I should come to work. I explained I was not feeling fine. They got angry with me and pushed me to come to work, but to no avail. I stood my ground and did not go out. Whatever would have happened that day, I do not and will never know.

One morning I was going to work at the Taiyuan normal college. When the taxi dropped me, I saw a man standing by the gate wearing a black jacket. I did not know what happened. Something within me warned me that that man might be dangerous. My intuition actually warned me. I dodged the front gate where the man was standing, went around, and entered the school through the back gate. I went into the classrooms and delivered my lessons. When I finished the lessons at noon, I left again through the back gate. Something kept telling me to be careful. I did not feel good about the man with the black jacket. Once I was out of the school and about to take a taxi, one of the best English students of the school rang my phone. I answered and she told me to come back, that there was something serious to discuss with me. I said no, I could not return. She pressed hard saying it was very important we talk. Moreover, she was a very good friend of mine. What would I do? I thought of the man with the black jacket. Might he be was the one calling for me now. Because she pressed so hard, I went back to re-enter the school.

Just as I was about to enter the gate, I met the man I had been dodging. The tall man, with well-developed and strong looking muscles, did not have a typical Chinese build. He was standing right there before me. He stopped me and asked "Hi shi shea?" meaning "Who are you?" He was frank in asking, an indication he was not out for any child's play. As soon as he posed the question, the gate man jumped forward and intervened. The gate man said, "Ta shi wai jao," meaning "He is the foreign teacher." When the gate man said this, I saw how the man turned around and withdrew.

I then moved forward and met the student who called for me. She told me she was very worried about a private problem. She had an American boyfriend. They had travelled together to the United States during the summer holiday. She told me she had just received a call from a relative of his who said her boyfriend was involved in an accident and that one of his legs would be amputated. She was so worried about this. You know, when the Chinese girls fall in love, deep inside their minds it is for nothing else but marriage. Most of them do not just fall in love to play around and go later. Even if they do not say it openly, when they are falling in love it is for marriage. Therefore, you can imagine what it meant for that student, that the leg of her future partner was to be amputated. She was wiping her tears as she spoke. She wanted someone to speak her mind to, and that is why she thought it wise to speak with me. I comforted her as much as a pastor could and went away. Whether it is for good or for bad, we are in it, that is all, what else. She later told me her boyfriend was playing a joke on her. I said that those kinds of jokes are difficult to imagine. A test? "I want to marry that girl, how can I test her loyalty to me?" and then a big lie comes like a bomb to someone's daughter. If this girl had no hypertension on that day, she will live long.

When I went home , I was still afraid because the students told me the man with the black jacket was a police officer. I asked my girlfriend to find out and tell me why a police officer was in the school that day. She found out and told me that students fought dangerously and attracted the attention of the police. She told me the police officer came to ensure that peace and security reigned in the school. My girlfriend never knew why I was afraid and asked her to find out things for me. She knew nothing concerning my visa problem.

As I worked, I hoped I might still find an opening one day to get my papers done. It was already quite some time since China had closed its borders, so I could not leave the country to return with an entry visa. Even by April 2008, there was not yet an opportunity to get my papers done. I did not know what to do. The security situation was getting worse. The communist government tightened security. Why in April 2008? Because the Olympic Games were near, and some of the sports would take place in my city – Taiyuan. Big preparations were underway for the Beijing Olympic Games which were to take place in August.

The police began serious checks on foreigners. They wanted to be sure all things were very ok before the games. The police went from class to class in search of foreign teachers. They went to all the homes where foreigners were known to live. Foreigners who had the least problem with their residential papers or visa were repatriated. There was no possibility to leave China for Mongolia or Macao to get another entry visa. China had to tighten its boarders before the Olympic Games. They did not want terrorists to come in and terrorize the Olympic community. China saw the Olympic Games as their pride. No idiot would make China fall. No one would try. To suffer in the hands of terrorists and immoral people was the last thing communist China would sit for. The government knew the pride of China could not fall. China was a very strong state and would stay strong. For these reasons, foreigners were well controlled. Where they lived, their places of work, and what exactly they were doing was very important. This made the police job easier in case there were problems.

The police had already arrested many foreigners who had no papers. Even those with papers that had expired just for a week or a few days before were arrested. Some foreigners who were only teaching about three hours a week were arrested. There I was teaching more than twenty hours a week in four different schools plus in many private classes. Would I survive the situation? I doubted it greatly. I was confused. Should I abandon work in all those schools and stay in my room? Even at home, it was not safe. Additionally, if I abandoned my jobs and stayed in my room, it meant I would lose my jobs. Then if by some luck I were still free in China after the games, I would have no job. I would have to start afresh looking for work, which was not that easy.

With all this in my head, I made a decision. I kept teaching in all the schools and kept on with my private classes as well. I decided I would not give up anything. One day I was in class teaching, and I received a message from a friend that the police arrested a foreigner. When I read the message, I was a little shaky but I decided to stand my ground. I went on with my class until the end. I went on with all my classes, and I did not abandon any. However, I stopped riding my bike and went around only in taxis to stay under cover. There were two police posts close to where I lived, so each time I left my apartment I took a taxi immediately, so I would not be spotted.

Then May 2008 came, and the situation got worse. It was not easy. The police kept arresting one foreigner after another. They intensified their search for foreigners. Despite all this, I vowed to teach my classes to the end. However, at this time, I also made the decision that I would return to Cameroon, pick up another entry visa, and return to China after the Olympic Games. If I returned in September, I would be able to continue work in all four schools where I worked. Thus there was a strong reason for me to work to the end, to protect my jobs, so that I could continue to work when I returned in September. June was approaching for the holidays to go into effect, and the security situation was very tense. The police were everywhere. It was not easy to get into schools and teach because the police might spot me. There were times my girlfriend had to go around and show me shortcuts to enter schools and teach.

My girlfriend kept assisting me in many ways, until one day she attended a party of many nationals. At that party, they were talking about Mr. Thomson. They said he came from Cameroon. My girlfriend knew Mr. Thomson and I were relatives. Then she thought, if he and I were relatives, how would he be a Cameroonian and I an American. The others at the party laughed at her. They went as far as telling her that my names were not the names of an American. She saw the truth in everything they said. She wept seriously, because she and I had planned to marry. To me, lying around everywhere was to find work, but I made the mistake and fell in love with her and had not yet told her my true nationality.

Every day I was thinking that when life got stable, I would inform her. Never did I imagine that the more I hid from her, the more disaster it would bring. When her parents attempted to warn her about me, she had openly told them she was going to marry me whether they wanted it or not. Now, with the new discovery, she got so confused. She saw how foolish she had been. She could not support it. She felt I had terribly betrayed her. My phone rang at 1 am. I saw it was her call. I picked up and she fired the question, "Are you American?" I knew it was serious as I heard her cry. However, I did not know what to say. She was weeping. At last, I spoke the truth, "No, I am not an American." This was terrible for her to bear. She met me in my apartment the next day and continued to weep and question. She finally settled with the idea that I was Cameroonian, and we continued to live together until the day I left China. However, during that time, I watched and observed that her mind was far off, never again deeply into the relationship as before.

I went on with all my jobs until the end of May. In early June, I finished teaching all my classes. Fortunately, nothing bad had happened. Because everything ended well in all my schools, in early June I told the authorities in all the schools that I was travelling abroad to return in September. I guaranteed them I would keep working on my return in September.

I was then planning seriously to leave China for Cameroon to pick up another entry visa. I was confused and did not know the steps. I sent my girlfriend with my identity card to the Cameroonian embassy in Beijing, to get me a laissez passé, in case I needed it. I could not go to Beijing myself because I would need to check into the bus or train with my passport. She left Taiyuan in the evening and arrived in Beijing in the morning. She went to the embassy, got the laissez passé, left Beijing in the evening, and arrived in Taiyuan in the morning. While in Beijing, she also went to the Beijing institute of traditional Chinese medicine and got my diploma, which they had prepared when I finished my studies just a week before. With my diploma in Chinese medicine, I knew that if I did not return to China, at least I would be able to practice herbal medicine and acupuncture with what I had learnt. She returned with one entire famous Beijing duck. She and I ate it up, and it was delectable.

What next, after my diploma and laissez passé in hand? Many people told me that if I reported myself to the police, they would keep me and I could not return to my apartment. Therefore, I decided to buy my airline ticket before going to the police station. It was June 6, so I bought my ticket with a scheduled departure on June 15, 2008. My girlfriend and I went and bought the ticket from Kenya Airways. Then on June 7, I packed my box, and my girlfriend and I went to the police. I carried the box with me in case the police would not let me return to my apartment. We arrived at the police station with my big box. My girlfriend told them I had come because my visa ran out, and I wanted to go home. She showed them my laissez passé and my flight ticket. They said the laissez passé was of no use, that they would follow the procedure they used in handling situations like mine.

The police chief looked at my passport and was angry. He said it was unacceptable to live in China for two years without a valid visa. He saw my big box standing there. He asked why I was carrying a box. My girlfriend told him it was my box. I told them that some friends had informed me that they would keep me in their station, so I decided to carry my box with me. To my surprise, they laughed. The police chief said they would keep me if I was unable to pay my fines for illegal stay. I told him I was ready to pay the fines. I paid the fine, and they told me to go home and to return to their station on June 12 to get an exit visa. My girlfriend and I returned on June 12 and got my passport. There was an "L" or tourist visa in it, issued on June 12 and marked valid until June 21.

My girlfriend and I returned home. We had mixed feelings. We were happy and sad at the same time. I had betrayed her. I was not American, but I was Cameroonian. We spent the next three days together. We vowed to reunite again and get married as we had planned. Then, the day of my departure came. The departure was from Guangzhou airport, far, far away from Taiyuan. Therefore, I had to leave Taiyuan on June 14 by bus and arrive in Guangzhou the next day. I was to leave Taiyuan by 11 am on the 14th. We left my apartment at 10 am for the bus station. The bus was there waiting. The driver and other passengers were already on board. Rong and I stood near the bus. We embraced. She could not let me go. I told her to be strong, that she must let go. It was not easy for her. It was not easy for me either, but I was leaving because I had no other option. I knew this very well, so I had to let her go by all means. Whether I liked it or not, I had to. I told her, "Be strong, be strong, let go." Then finally, she let hold of me. She turned and began to go. I stood watching her, as I repeated to her in my mind, "Go, go, go…"

Conclusion

L ife is a mystery. It unfolds in many ways. Never say die. Never give up. What I experienced in Cameroon and in China taught me that a man, a woman should be ready for anything at any time. It is difficult to know what is on the way, the next minute, hour, day, week, month, not to talk of coming years. Much good happens with time, and much of what we call evil. In life, ask yourself, "Am I ready for the good and the bad that will inevitably happen in the next second, the next minute, the next hour, the next day, the next month, the next year and so on?" If the answer is no, then you had better strengthen yourself in whatever way you can and get ready. Are you ready to face the future for good or for bad? Are you ready to sustain an emergency without asking why it happened in the first place? If big gains fall on your lap tomorrow, do not get overjoyed, but at least be happy and contented. If you suffer a big loss tomorrow, do not let grief kill you because the loss will pass. Life is like that. When the pendulum swings to the far end of negativities, be calm and patient, wait and act. It will eventually swing back into positivity, fortune and wellbeing. Life is like this, with these swings back and forth. One swing one way depending on the nature of the problem, how deeply rooted it is, may take just a few days or weeks to swing back to the positive end. However, some very difficult situations may take months and even years. Nevertheless, one thing is certain, that life must swing to the other end. So if you know that it must swing to the other end no matter how long it takes, why not wait. So too, when life is good, you should prepare yourself for times when things might not be so good. That is the way I see life. In difficult times, look around and see what you are gaining. When things are not going the way you expect, look around and see what you are learning. I am saying all this because despite the unstable life I lived in China, I was learning many new things that I would not have learnt without my travels there. I will not discourage any human being from adventures. Many times adventures pay off and change your life in a way you never expected. Looking deeply into life, you will automatically see that all life is adventure. Observe what happens when you set up minor and major plans you want to accomplish. You will observe that many things come in between. Those are already the unexpected (the adventures) that you have to manage. Promise to take heart and hope, hope, and hope, and hope does not fail!